"Lamott shows how she puts her religion into action . . . She succeeds in turning her stories on daily life into emotionally charged facts readers can hold on to." —*St. Petersburg Times*

"Her eye for human detail—the beauty of the mundane, especially describing the glue that holds families together—is keen and touching." —*The Seattle Times*

"Five years after her bestselling *Traveling Mercies*, Lamott sends us twenty-four fresh dispatches from the frontier of her life and her Christian faith. To hear her tell it, neither the state of the country nor the state of her nerves has improved, to say the least. *Plan B* is better than brilliant. This is that rare kind of book that is like having a smart, dear, crazy (in the best sense) friend walk next to us in sunlight and in the dark night of the soul." —*Publishers Weekly*

"Brilliant bits of Lamott's witty, profound observations about life—this one and the hereafter . . . Readers didn't have to be new parents, recovering alcoholics, or religious to appreciate Lamott's struggles—existential and otherwise—through her first year with Sam. And they don't need to be any of those things to enjoy the sometimes hilarious and ever-candid revelations about the profundity of everyday living Lamott proffers in *Plan B* . . . What bubbles to the surface of *Plan B*—a wonderful, wise bundle of her characteristically blithe prose sure to become a bestseller—will tickle funny bones and enliven spirits." —*Chicago Sun-Times*

"[A] rich collection of personal essays . . . plainspoken, direct, even gritty. As always, surprising twists lurk in her prose. Some provide sudden hilarity, others reveal searing insights . . . her writing is fresh and earthy, clean and comforting."

—*St. Louis Post-Dispatch*

"Annie tackles tough subjects in this book . . . they include the enormously politicized and simultaneously intensely personal modern Christianity. She does this with insight, verve, and a decidedly liberal outlook. This is refreshing in a time when Christianity has been claimed (some would say 'stolen') by right-wingers. You show 'em, Annie. There is much our country could absorb from an aging, loving, liberal crank from Marin County who once started a Sunday school even though 'it turned out that I did not like children, or at any rate, they made me extremely nervous, and I had almost nothing to share with them, except that Jesus loved them, and I did, too, even when I was in a bad mood.'"

—*The San Jose Mercury News*

"Lamott's uncanny ease at applying wit, passion, and self-deprecation to Big, Important Subjects—politics, religion, parenthood, alcoholism, her mother's death after a battle with Alzheimer's—lends *Plan B* vital warmth that is the perfect antidote to preachiness. Lamott employs cheerfully loopy logic to problems, is never too shy to pray, and remains brutally honest about her failings. We definitely owe her thanks. Just like her other works, *Plan B* brings joy indeed."

—*The Miami Herald*

continued . . .

"[Lamott's] brilliance as a spiritual writer lies in her willingness to acknowledge the moments when it seems that faith can't keep up with the bleakness and sorrow of ordinary life. Lamott keeps trying to lead a good life, even when that involves doing things that don't come easily, such as starting a Sunday school for kids at her church or wearing an outfit for a friend's wedding that makes her look like Dame Edna. In these essays, we're to understand that the world is still full of heartbreaking possibility. In the best of Lamott's pieces, we're ready to believe it, yet again."

—*The Cleveland Plain Dealer*

"Knock-you-flat insight memorable for its earthiness and rightness."   —*The Albany Times Union*

"*Plan B* is grade-A. Lamott is one of our most gifted observers of the human condition. I could not put the book down until I had savored every splendid sentence. The tears of laughter and rage dot every page."   —*Dayton Daily News*

"In Lamott's world, faith isn't something a person should rely on only for matters of life and death; faith provides fortification that is just as crucial during a mother's daily battles with her son over chores and homework. *Plan B* is an amusing, refreshing discussion of the practical matters of faith and religion that is welcome at a time when the debate of such topics often leads to histrionic factionalism."—*Rocky Mountain News*

Plan B

further thoughts on faith

anne lamott

riverhead books

New York

THE BERKLEY PUBLISHING GROUP
Published by the Penguin Group
Penguin Group (USA) Inc.
375 Hudson Street, New York, New York 10014, USA
Penguin Group (Canada), 90 Eglinton Avenue East, Suite 700, Toronto, Ontario M4P 2Y3, Canada
(a division of Pearson Penguin Canada Inc.)
Penguin Books Ltd., 80 Strand, London WC2R 0RL, England
Penguin Group Ireland, 25 St. Stephen's Green, Dublin 2, Ireland (a division of Penguin Books Ltd.)
Penguin Group (Australia), 250 Camberwell Road, Camberwell, Victoria 3124, Australia
(a division of Pearson Australia Group Pty. Ltd.)
Penguin Books India Pvt. Ltd., 11 Community Centre, Panchsheel Park, New Delhi—110 017, India
Penguin Group (NZ), cnr Airborne and Rosedale Roads, Albany, Auckland 1310, New Zealand
(a division of Pearson New Zealand Ltd.)
Penguin Books (South Africa) (Pty.) Ltd., 24 Sturdee Avenue, Rosebank, Johannesburg 2196,
South Africa

Penguin Books Ltd., Registered Offices: 80 Strand, London WC2R 0RL, England

First Riverhead hardcover edition: March 2005
First Riverhead trade paperback edition: April 2006
Riverhead trade paperback ISBN: 1-59448-157-1

The Library of Congress has catalogued the Riverhead hardcover edition as follows:

Lamott, Anne.
Plan B : further thoughts on faith / Anne Lamott.
p.   cm.
ISBN 1-57322-299-2
1. Lamott, Anne—Religion.   2. Novelists, American—20th century—Biography.   3. Christian
biography—United States.   4. Faith.   I. Title.
PS3562.A4645Z467   2005   2004051391
813'.54—dc22
[B]

PRINTED IN THE UNITED STATES OF AMERICA

10   9   8   7   6   5   4   3   2   1

For Rory

I am deeply grateful to David Talbot, editor in chief of Salon.com, who published much of this material in earlier form. I am just about the only overtly spiritual person he can stand, but even so he has always given me absolute freedom and unwavering support. Lori Leibovich, my editor at Salon, has shown me total patience, friendship, and great editing.

My friends are the reason I have so much faith in God, and I owe special thanks to the people who help me with my work: Neshama Franklin, Tom Weston, Mark Childress, Geneen Roth, Doug Foster, and Anne Huffington. And thank you, Karl Fleming, for your faith in me, and your letters saying so. I tape them to the wall beside my desk. Robyn Posin, where would I be without you?

Cindy Spiegel at Riverhead is a great, challenging editor and friend. Anna Jardine is a tough, cool, reputation-saving copy editor.

I would be grateful even to know someone who is as both loving and savvy as Sarah Chalfant, and here she's my *agent*—along with the incomparable Andrew Wylie.

And I would not be here were it not for the love, support, and wisdom of the people of St. Andrew Presbyterian Church, Marin City, California, and the Reverend Ms. Veronica Goines. Their deep faith and love of God, and life, have changed my world forever: they taught me by their witness that no matter how hard life seems at times, we can still—in the words of Warren Zevon—enjoy every sandwich; and give thanks.

contents

monet refuses the operation

Doctor, you say there are no halos
around the streetlights in Paris
and what I see is an aberration
caused by old age, an affliction.
I tell you it has taken me all my life
to arrive at the vision of gas lamps as angels,
to soften and blur and finally banish
the edges you regret I don't see,
to learn that the line I called the horizon
does not exist and sky and water,
so long apart, are the same state of being.
Fifty-four years before I could see
Rouen cathedral is built
of parallel shafts of sun,
and now you want to restore
my youthful errors: fixed
notions of top and bottom,
the illusion of three-dimensional space,
wisteria separate
from the bridge it covers.
What can I say to convince you
the Houses of Parliament dissolve
night after night to become

the fluid dream of the Thames?
I will not return to a universe
of objects that don't know each other,
as if islands were not the lost children
of one great continent. The world
is flux, and light becomes what it touches,
becomes water, lilies on water,
above and below water,
becomes lilac and mauve and yellow
and white and cerulean lamps,
small fists passing sunlight
so quickly to one another
that it would take long, streaming hair
inside my brush to catch it.
To paint the speed of light!
Our weighted shapes, these verticals,
burn to mix with air
and change our bones, skin, clothes
to gases. Doctor,
if only you could see
how heaven pulls earth into its arms
and how infinitely the heart expands
to claim this world, blue vapor without end.

—LISEL MUELLER

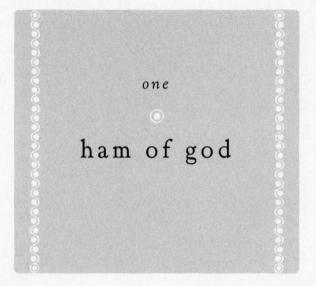

one

ham of god

On my forty-ninth birthday, I decided that all of life was hopeless, and I would eat myself to death. These are desert days. Better to go out by our own hands than to endure slow death by scolding at the hands of the Bush administration. However, after a second cup of coffee, I realized that I couldn't kill myself that morning—not because it was my birthday but because I'd promised to get arrested the next day. I had been arrested three weeks earlier with an ecumenical bunch of religious peaceniks, people who still believe in Dr. King and Gandhi. Also, my back was out. I didn't want to die in crone mode. Plus, there was no food in the house. So I took a long, hot shower instead and began another day of being gloated to death.

Everyone I know has been devastated by Bush's presidency and, in particular, our country's heroic military activities overseas. I can usually manage a crabby hope that there is meaning in mess and pain, that more will be revealed, and that truth and beauty will somehow win out in the end. But I'd been struggling as my birthday approached. So much had been stolen from us by Bush, from the very beginning of his reign, and especially since he went to war in Iraq. I wake up some mornings pinned to the bed by centrifugal sadness and frustration. A friend called to wish me Happy Birthday, and I remembered something she'd said many years ago, while reading a *Vanity Fair* article about Hitler's affair with his niece. "I have *had* it with Hitler," Peggy said vehemently, throwing the magazine to the floor. And I'd had it with Bush.

Hadn't the men in the White House ever heard of the word *karma*? They lied their way into taking our country to war, crossing another country's borders with ferocious military might, trying to impose our form of government on a sovereign nation, without any international agreement or legal justification, and set about killing the desperately poor on behalf of the obscenely rich. Then we're instructed, like naughty teenagers, to refrain from saying that it was an immoral war that set a disastrous precedent— because to do so is to offer aid and comfort to the enemy.

While I was thinking about all this, my Jesuit friend Father Tom called. He is one of my closest friends, a few years older than I, a scruffy aging Birkenstock type, like me, who gives lectures and leads retreats on spirituality. Usually he calls to report on the latest rumors of my mental deterioration, drunkenness, or promiscuity, how sick it makes everyone to know that I am showing all my lady parts to the neighbors. But this time he called to wish me Happy Birthday.

"How are we going to get through this craziness?" I asked. There was silence for a moment.

"Left foot, right foot, left foot, breathe," he said.

Father Tom loves the desert. A number of my friends do. They love the skies that pull you into infinity, like the ocean. They love the silence, and how, if you listen long enough, the pulse of the desert begins to sound like the noise your finger makes when you run it around the rim of a crystal glass. They love the scary beauty—snakes, lizards, scorpions, the kestrels and hawks. They love the mosaics of water-washed pebbles on the desert floor, small rocks that cast huge shadows, a shoot of vegetation here, a wildflower there.

I like the desert for short periods of time, from inside a car, with the windows rolled up and the doors locked. I prefer beach resorts with room service. But liberals have been in the desert for several years now, and I'm worn out. Some days I hardly know what to pray for. Peace? Well, whatever.

So the morning of my birthday, because I couldn't pray, I did what Matisse once said to do: "I don't know if I believe in God or not. . . . But the essential thing is to put oneself in a frame of mind which is close to that of prayer." I closed my eyes, and got quiet. I tried to look like Mother Mary, with dreadlocks and a bad back.

But within seconds, I was frantic to turn on the TV. I was in withdrawal—I needed more scolding from Donald Rumsfeld, and more malignant celebration of what everyone agreed, in April 2003, was a great victory for George W. Bush. So we couldn't find those stupid weapons of mass destruction—pick, pick, pick. I didn't turn on the TV. I kept my eyes closed, and breathed. I started to feel crazy, and knew that all I needed was five minutes of CNN. I listened to the birds sing outside, and it was like Chinese water torture, which I am sure we don't say anymore. Then I remembered the weekend when 11 million people in the world marched for peace, how joyful it was to be part of the stirrings of a great movement. My pastor, Veronica, says that peace is joy at rest, and joy is peace on its feet, and I felt both that weekend.

I lay on the floor with my eyes closed for so long that my dog, Lily, came over and worriedly licked me back to life. That cheered me up. "What did you get me for my birthday?" I asked. She started to chew on my head. That helped. Maybe the old left is dead, but after we've rested awhile we can prepare for something new. I don't know who on the left can lead us away from the craziness and barbarity: I'm very confused now. But I know that in the desert, you stay out of the blistering sun. You go out during the early morning, and in the cool of the evening. You seek oasis, shade, safety, refreshment. There's every hue of green, and of gold. But I'm only pretending to think it's beautiful; I find it terribly scary. I walk on eggshells, and hold my breath.

I called Tom back.

He listened quietly. I asked him for some good news.

He thought. "Well," he said finally. "My cactuses are blooming. Last week they were ugly and reptilian, and now they are bursting with red and pink blossoms. They don't bloom every year, so you have to love them while they're here."

"I hate cactuses," I said. "I want to know what to do. Where we even start."

"We start by being kind to ourselves. We breathe, we eat. We remember that God is present wherever people suffer. God's here with us when we're miserable, and God is there in Iraq. The suffering of innocent people draws God close to them. Kids hit by U.S. bombs are not abandoned by God."

"Well, it sure looks like they were," I said. "It sure looks that way to their parents."

"It also looked like Christ had been abandoned on the cross. It looked like a win for the Romans."

"How do we help? How do we not lose our minds?"

"You take care of the suffering."

"I can't get to Iraq."

"There are folks who are miserable here."

After we got off the phone, I ate a few birthday chocolates. Then I asked God to help me be helpful. It was the first time that day that I felt my prayers were sent, and then received—like e-mail. I tried to cooperate with grace, which is to say, I did not turn on the TV. I asked God to help me again. The problem with God—or at any rate, one of the top five most annoying things about God—is that He or She rarely answers right away. It can take days, weeks. Some people seem to understand this—that life and change take time. Chou En-lai, when asked, "What do you think of the French Revolution?" paused for a minute—smoking incessantly—then replied, "Too soon to tell." I, on the other hand, am an instant-message type. It took decades for Bush to destroy the Iraqi army in three weeks.

But I prayed: Help me. And then I drove to the market in silence, to buy my birthday dinner.

I flirted with everyone in the store, especially the old people, and I lightened up. When the checker finished ringing up my items, she looked at my receipt and cried, "Hey! You've won a ham!"

I felt blindsided by the news. I had asked for help, not a ham. This was very disturbing. What on earth was I going to do with ten pounds of salty pink eraser? I rarely eat it. It makes you bloat.

"Wow," I said. The checker was so excited about giving it to me that I pretended I was, too.

How great!

A bagger was dispatched to the back of the store to fetch my ham. I stood waiting anxiously. I wanted to go home, so I could start caring for suffering people, or turn on CNN. I almost suggested that the checker award the ham to the next family who paid with food stamps. But for some reason, I waited. If God was giving me a ham, I'd be crazy not to receive it. Maybe it was the ham of God, who takes away the sins of the world.

I waited ten minutes for what I began to think of as "that fucking ham." Finally the bag boy handed me a parcel the size of a cat. I put it with feigned cheer into my grocery cart, and walked to the car, trying to figure out who might need it. I thought about chucking the parcel out the window near a field. I was so distracted that I crashed my cart smack into a slow-moving car in the parking lot.

I started to apologize, when I noticed that the car was a rusty wreck, and that an old friend was at the wheel. We got sober together a long time ago, and each of us had a son at the same time. She has dark black skin and processed hair the color of cooled tar.

She opened her window. "Hey," I said. "How are you—it's my birthday!"

"Happy Birthday," she said, and started crying. She looked drained and pinched, and after a moment, she pointed to her gas gauge. "I don't have money for gas, or food. I've never asked for help from a friend since I got sober, but I'm asking you to help me."

"I've got money," I said.

"No, no, I just need gas," she said. "I've never asked someone for a handout."

"It's not a handout," I told her. "It's my birthday present." I thrust a bunch of money into her hand, everything I had. Then I reached into my shopping cart and held out the ham to her like a clown offering flowers. "Hey!" I said. "Do you and your kids like ham?"

"We love it," she said. "We love it for every meal."

She put it in the seat beside her, firmly, lovingly, as if she were about to strap it in. And she cried some more.

Later, thinking about her, I remembered the seasonal showers in the desert, how potholes in the rocks fill up with rain. When you look later, there are already frogs in the water, and brine shrimp reproducing, like commas doing the macarena; and it seems, but only seems, that you went from parched to overflow in the blink of an eye.

two

◉

red cords

I wear something on my wrist that one would not expect a Presbyterian woman to wear: a thin red cotton cord that was blessed by the Dalai Lama, and given to me by my Buddhist friend Jack Kornfield. It's quite ratty, with what look like rings of laundry lint circling it. I separate these rings with my thumbnail when I am fidgety, as if counting with the beads of an abacus.

Jack and I take walks every few weeks, when we are both in town, often in the hills above the meditation center he founded nearby. He teaches his students, and has taught me, to slow down, breathe, and take care of everyone, which is of course the same message Jesus taught—that breath is our connection to holy spirit, to our bodies, minds, and soul; and that if the devil can't get you to sin, he'll keep you busy. Jack is about my age and height, slight and very Jewish: he brought me homemade chicken soup last time I was sick in bed. He also seems vaguely East Indian, smooth and brown, and gives off a light, spicy, ancient smell.

Breathing has never been my strong suit. I've never been very good at breathing. When I was young, I was afraid that if I stopped remembering to breathe, I'd have cardiac arrest. I was always much better at holding my breath for long periods of time, the length of the pool, or of the tunnel that leads to the Golden Gate Bridge. At the age of two, I used to hold my breath in public until I passed out. My first memory is of coming to on the planks of the boardwalk in Tiburon, my father nudging me from way high up, with his shoe. Then he reached down kindly and pulled me back to my feet. He had been dead several years before his sister told me that he used to hold his breath and pass out on the streets of Tokyo, where his parents were Presbyterian missionaries. I think he was a little angry: held breath is the ultimate withholding; you're not taking anything in, you're not putting anything out.

I am a little angry, too. I feel that we began witnessing the end of the world in Super SloMo once George W. Bush became president, and some days it takes everything I can muster not to lose my hope, my faith, and myself. One out of six women in my area is now being diagnosed with breast cancer. My son is in his teens, and I am in menopause: I have not felt this clueless and tired since Sam was a colicky baby. We are both more testy now on a regular basis, quicker to anger, and in my case, to weep and reevaluate the meaning of life. Sometimes I feel like the big possum who has been coming into our driveway lately, worried and waddly. I hear that the stress hormones possums produce are off the charts. Possums live only a few years in the wild. I suppose that if I had two penises and still fainted a lot, I'd be stressed to the max, too.

I am fifty, and have only now figured out why you are supposed to have babies when you are young: so that by the time your child is in his teens, one of you is stable some of the time, and you the mother are not racked with back pain and Alzheimer's. Sam has grown tall and muscular. I have grown wider, stiff, and achy. I trip a lot and hit my head on cabinets I forgot were there. I get into the shower with my glasses on. And whereas I always had a slim waist, I suddenly have two stomachs—a regular tummy and another one below that, which I call the subcontinent. This older body is both amazingly healthy and a big disappointment.

Jack knotted a number of blessings into my cord last year when he tied it on my wrist, to protect me from the values and judgment of the world, from the disaster of my own thinking, and to allow me the forgetting of myself. I tug at the red cord constantly: it was an anointing of sorts, and I will take all the anointing I can get. My pastor, Veronica, explained recently that in the Twenty-third Psalm, when David says that his Shepherd anointed his head with oil, it referred to the fragrant oil a shepherd would put around his sheep's mouths to prevent an infestation of flies. Otherwise, the flies would lay their eggs in the soft tissues of the sheep's mouths, and when the eggs hatched, the sheep would go crazy, butting their heads against trees to dislodge the infestation. When my head is filled with worries and resentments, the cord helps me remember that I was anointed. I am safe, even when my cup is not exactly runneth-ing over.

I used my red string as an audiovisual aid last Sunday when I got to give the sermon at church. First I walked around, letting everyone see it. Then I spoke briefly about the red cords that gave us life, that connect us to our sources: the image of Christ's blood, and the umbilical cord that stretched from my mother to me, and from Sam to me, cords carrying life. Then I moved on to the story of Rahab, from Joshua 2 in the Hebrew Bible, whose life was saved by a red cord. She was one of the bad girls of the Old Testament, a prostitute in Jericho, at the end of the Israelites' wilderness journey. Joshua was their leader, Moses' anointed successor. When Rahab's story begins, Joshua and his army are camped on the River Jordan across from Jericho, which they are about to invade. He sends two spies into Jericho to find out how strong the opposing army is.

The spies want to blend in, so they go to stay with Rahab, the most infamous prostitute of her time, figuring that if they go to the local Travelodge, they'll stick out, but that at Rahab's, half the men in town will be there, and no one will notice them or say anything. It is like, "If I see you in New Orleans, I won't see you in New Orleans."

Rahab lives in an apartment built just inside the walls of Jericho, like a Pueblo or Anasazi dwelling; her windows are built into the outside wall.

The king's spies visit Rahab's—on official business, no doubt—and report to him that Joshua's spies are staying with her. The king sends his soldiers to Rahab's to demand that she turn over Joshua's spies.

But word has it that the Israelites are under the protection of a loving God: everyone has heard about the Red Sea's parting, and that God has cared for the Israelites in the harsh desert for forty years. In that dark and scary time, with war about to break out, and no standing in her own community, Rahab feels something in her heart that tells her to align herself with the people of God. So she lies to the king's soldiers, and says that by the time the gate to the city was closed at dark the night before, the spies had already gotten away. Actually, she hid them on her roof, in stalks of flax.

Why did she hide them, since, by the calculus of the world, that act endangered her?

She did it because she was desperate, and so she listened to her heart. In my experience, there is a lot to be said for desperation—not exactly a bright side, but something expressed in words for which "God" could be considered an acronym: gifts of desperation. The main gift is a willingness to give up the conviction that you are right, and that God thinks so, too, and hates the people who are driving you crazy. Something spoke to Rahab through her heart, or through what Mel Brooks, in "The 2,000 Year

Old Man," refers to as the broccoli: "Listen to your broccoli, and your broccoli will tell you how to eat it."
Something told Rahab that if she aligned herself with the
people who had been brought so far by faith, she would
be safe as well. This gave her the radical conviction that
she should be cared for. Rahab believed that God was trying to get her attention, and she listened.

I try to listen for God's voice inside me, but my sense
of discernment tends to be ever so slightly muddled.
When God wants to get my attention, She clears Her
throat a number of times, trying to get me to look up, or
inward—and then if I don't pay attention, She rolls Her
eyes, makes a low growling sound, and starts kicking me
under the table with Her foot.

Rahab got the spies of the Israelites to swear that if she
didn't rat them out, they would spare her and her family.

She let the spies out the window and down the wall by
rope. And they gave her a red cord to tie in the window.
They returned to tell Joshua their news; and Joshua
moved his great army across the Jordan and, in the words
of the old spiritual, fit the battle of Jericho. And the walls
came a-tumblin' down.

But Joshua's soldiers saw the scarlet cord in Rahab's
window, and spared those she had gathered inside, and all

because she turned to the spirit within her, the secret place that, as Robert Frost wrote, "sits in the middle and knows." She went on to live a life of great honor, marrying an Israelite and becoming one of the four women mentioned in Matthew's genealogy from Abraham to David to Jesus.

You've got to love this in a God—consistently assembling the motleyest people to bring, into the lonely and frightening world, a commitment to caring and community. It's a centuries-long reality show—Moses the stutterer, Rahab the hooker, David the adulterer, Mary the homeless teenager. Not to mention all the mealy-mouthed disciples. Not to mention a raging insecure narcissist like me.

When I finished my sermon last Sunday, everyone clapped like mad, and I felt like Miss Spiritual America, with a red cord and an invisible tiara. I greeted everyone after the service with humility, ducking my head shyly and all but pawing the ground with my foot. A few of the older women teared up when they thanked me, remembering the wreck I'd been when I first started coming to St. Andrew, a year before I got sober.

Then I went home and had a huge fight with Sam.

It's hard to imagine things can get so ugly so quickly, just because the word "homework" has come up, but they do. I was savoring my morning in church, while making us sandwiches, when Sam innocently mentioned in passing that his science report was due the next day, but he had left his binder in his locker at school, and would automatically be docked a grade for lateness. He'd had a month to complete the assignment, he'd given me his word that he was on top of it, and I was furious.

I spluttered and fumed in the kitchen, and stormed down the hall to my own room, like a Cossack—or like my mother used to do when she headed down the hall to my older brother's room to bellow at him because he hadn't done his homework. I would flatten myself against the wall and stop breathing, or huddle in my younger brother's room, trying to distract him from the chaos.

Sam shouted that I was turning out like my mother. He can always find the soft parts of me, where there is no turtle shell for protection.

I slammed the door and started hitting it with my fist. Then I lay facedown on the bed. The kitty tried to comfort me but accidentally started chewing the red cord off my wrist. Jack came into my mind. What would he do?

It's hard to tell with him. Once I called to say hello, and he was making liver and onions. Usually he suggests that I be kind, and breathe, and take a walk. So I did.

It was drizzling outside, but I was so miserable and without a plan that I put on a raincoat, called Lily, my dog, and headed outside to the open-space hills behind my house. I go up there almost every day with Lily. It is a quiet and holy space. My family scattered my mother's ashes there last year, two years after she died: it had taken me that long to stop being mad at her, for having been such a mess my whole life. On the hillside is a mysterious concrete piling where I like to sit when there is dew on the ground, or a mist, so my pants won't get wet. I have a 360-degree view of my town and the mountain and the foothills. In the early morning, I can see the sun rise above the nearest suburb, and when I come at dusk, the sun sets out toward the farmlands of rural Marin and the Pacific Ocean. Your senses are bathed in smells and sounds and visions, whether you want to receive or not, because the only walls are the tall eucalyptus to the east. You feel unprotected and small and buffeted by the wind, and this defenselessness is a crack through which fresh air and water can enter.

I sat on the piling. The drizzle had stopped, but the air was still moist—a warm, windy spring evening. The willows, hectic in the wind, were sticklike and gray, their leaves not quite out, yet you could feel them pushing through.

I fiddled with my red cord, separating the rings of laundry lint: I can't figure out how these rings could have formed on the cord, as I have never removed it; still, there are three knots, and seven rings of lint.

When he finished tying it, Jack said that the cord was my new transcript. "You have gotten an A-plus, Annie, for your work during this life." But Jack feels this way about everyone, and it almost ruins it for me that he thinks we are all doing so well with such difficult material as being alive, having parents, kids, bodies, minds, certain presidents.

All wise people say the same thing: that you are deserving of love, and that it's all here now, everything you need. There's the memoir by a Hindu writer, *It's Here Now (Are You?),* and one of my priest friends says the exact same thing, so I think it must be true—that when you pray, you are not starting the conversation from scratch, just remembering to plug back into a conversation that's always in progress.

There I sat on the hill, hands folded in my lap, eyes closed, and I started to relax. But then I made a cardinal mistake: I started to think about how holy I was acting, in the face of teenage contempt and shirking; how grown-up, spiritually, emotionally. And this pleased me.

And it was bad.

It was like, "Batter up!"

First the dogs arrived, three of them, from out of nowhere, barking at Lily and me until their owner stepped into the clearing and commanded them to be quiet. I smiled and waved, but closed my eyes so that she could see that I was in holiness mode. "It's windy!" she cried. I opened my eyes. She had a walking stick, and looked like a shepherd, of bad dogs.

"What's your dog's name?" she shouted. I told her. "What kind of dog is she? *Where'd she get those ears? Here, Lily! Here, girl.*" The woman sounded like someone from the shouting Loud family, on the old *Saturday Night Live.*

I hung my head and smiled to myself.

"I forgot your name," she shouted. I told her, and she waved and headed down the hillside. I closed my eyes, breathed in calm, and grass; and then, the pièce de résis-

tance: the smell of dog shit filled my nose, sharp as ammonia, and foul.

God, I thought, self-righteously: This woman brings her barking dogs into this open space, and they shit all over everything, and she doesn't clean up after them. I stood to move away, but when I looked down at the grass, there was nothing there. Then I looked at the sole of my shoe.

My entire childhood passed before my eyes—kids holding their noses in schoolyards, parents commanding us all out of the car, demanding that we check our feet. Nothing isolated you so instantly as having stinky heatlines wafting visibly off your foot, like in the cartoons.

It's a miracle that more of us didn't shoot up our neighborhoods.

When I was young, I wore camel's-hair coats when I took the bus to San Francisco with my mother to see the dentist, and then drown our sorrows in coffee-toffee cake at Blum's. Back then everyone dressed up to go to the city. I wore patent-leather shoes and white gloves. I had a felt hat, with a red grosgrain ribbon around the brim, and tucked into that, a feather: can you imagine? Sam would die laughing if he could see how I dressed, like a rebel-

lious Amish girl. But I felt so beautiful. However, not
even finery, not even *feathers,* could protect you from dog
shit. You'd instantly be stuck in a game of Chutes and
Ladders, feeling beautiful and proud one moment, people
holding their noses the next.

I got up and pawed the offending shoe against the wet
grass, then sat down on the concrete piling and looked at
my shoe. There was an enormous amount of doggage
embedded in its elaborate treads.

Muttering, I searched for a stick in the grass, and once
I found one, started picking out the shit, but it was pebbly, and stuck. Trying to dislodge it was like picking burnt
batter out of a waffle iron.

It took forever. Then a light drizzle started up again. I
kept at the sneaker, and two things happened: First, the
project turned out to be strangely satisfying—I'm really
good at this sort of work. And second, after a while I
found myself in a state of joy. I was focused, and it was
beautiful up there, and the shit was nearly entirely out of
my shoe. That's a lot. I don't know why God won't just
spritz away our hardships and frustration. I don't know
why the most we can hope for on some days is to end up
a little less crazy than before, less down on ourselves. I
don't know why we have to become so vulnerable before

we can connect with God, and even sometimes with ourselves. But by the same token, I don't understand how I
got rings of laundry lint on my red cord.

I guess we're simply not meant to understand some
things. Bono, of U2, who is a Christian, says that his
favorite song is "Amazing Grace" and his second favorite
is "Help Me Make It Through the Night," and most of
the time, I have to let it go at that.

I prayed for Sam and me. And then I called for Lily
and headed back home in the drizzle.

I took off my shoes outside the front door, because I
wanted to wash the soles off. Sam's shoes were on the
front step, too, so muddy and worn that you might expect
to find just one of them, at a flood site, or at low tide. This
is how the guys wear them.

Sam was lying on the couch watching TV when I
stepped in. I could tell he was still mad, because for a
moment he did not look over. I closed the door behind me.

"I'm sorry I was awful," I said. "I don't know what's
wrong with me sometimes. Everything gets to be too
much, and I can't breathe."

He looked over in wounded silence. Then, as he actually saw me, there was an almost imperceptible shift in his
face, as when he was a baby, first waking from a deep

sleep: you could see his inside eyes open before he blinked awake, as if something inside him had floated to the surface from far away. "Look at you," he said, amused, parental. "You're all wet. Where you been? And where on earth are your *shoes,* dude?" Then he rubbed his forehead, wearily, but smiling, just like my mother used to do.

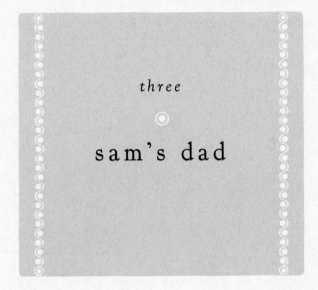

three

sam's dad

We have recently returned from another holiday with Sam's dad. It feels like a miracle to be able to say that, and it feels that way every time his father and I spend time together with Sam, watching him ski or draw or sleep. Because for me to be able to write that first sentence seemed, for the first seven years of Sam's life, an impossibility. I want to tell you the story now, of how Sam and his father met, because in these dark and scary times, it always makes me feel hope again. I've said this before: When God is going to do something wonderful, He or She always starts with a hardship; when

God is going to do something amazing, He or She starts with an impossibility.

I have written about being a single mother but have rarely mentioned Sam's father, except in a memoir of Sam's first year, where I said things that made me sound perhaps a little victimized by and merciless toward his father. In early December 1988, I got pregnant by a man named John, whom I had been dating, in the biblical sense. We did not sit around all day making moo-goo-gai-pan eyes at each other, but we hung out and loved to talk and go to movies and libraries. It was very nice. Then I got pregnant, and John, who already had two grown children, was ready for independence and travel, while I was ready to have a baby. I was thirty-four and could not face more abortions, and my eggs were getting old, like eggs you'd get at the 7-Eleven. I decided to have the baby, and everything between John and me turned to shit, and he went his way and I went mine.

Then I had this beautiful kid. It was very hard in the beginning, and I hated that Sam didn't get to have a dad, but I provided him with the world's kindest men. I didn't even think of trying to find John, this man with whom I had such a bad history, yet who'd given me the greatest gift of my life.

When Sam asked about his father over the years, which was not often, I'd tell him the truth. Sort of. I did not mention how badly things had ended, that his dad and I had said things to each other that perhaps Jesus would not have said. I told Sam what a smart, sweet man his father was, which is true, that he was tall and good-looking. I told him I had two photos of John he could see if he ever wanted to, and that I'd help him if he ever wanted to try to find him. And I really, really hoped he'd never want to.

When Sam was in first grade, there was a fine crack in the wall of silence. A letter arrived from John, in response to a story I'd published about Sam and his first library card. It was one sentence of grief and pride and outreach—but there was no phone number or other way to contact him. It only made me feel more confused, and in my swirl of blame and fear, I put the letter away.

A year later, when Sam was seven, he started wondering more frequently where his dad was, and what kind of a man he was. The man I was with at the time told me point-blank that I had to help Sam begin his search. That it was time. I wept. I was so afraid—sore afraid—and hopeless that Sam would never get to find his father or that, even worse, he would.

When Sam would ask about his father, I'd say, "Do you want to see his pictures?" He always said no, thank you. (He has good manners, which I believe can cover a multitude of sins.) But one day when we were sitting in the car after church, he looked solemn. Clearly he had something on his mind. He said, "I think I'd like to see those pictures now."

I felt as if I had swallowed a bunch of rubber bands. When we got home, I took the photos out of the file and handed them to Sam. He studied John for a moment, the big round eyes, small nose, dark hair, all like his own.

"How could we find him?" he asked.

I didn't know, except that with writing, you start where you are, and you usually do it poorly. You just do it—you do it afraid. And something happens.

I called John's old number, the one in the phone book, and no one answered. I called John's father's house, and no one answered there. I called his best friend, with whom I had lost touch, and there was no one there, either. Then I prayed, because when all else fails, you follow instructions, and I began to pray the way my mentors had taught me: I prayed, "Help me, help me." I prayed, "Please. Please." I let go of an angstrom of blame. That was the hardest part. This batch of blame had more claw marks than most of the things I try to let go of. Blame is always my first response: figure out whose fault things are, and then try to manipulate that person into correcting his or her behavior so that you can be more comfortable. I put a note to God in a box, asking for direction. I told God I was taking my sticky fingers off the steering wheel, that God could be the driver and I would be just another bozo on the bus.

"Help" is a prayer that is always answered. It doesn't matter how you pray—with your head bowed in silence, or crying out in grief, or dancing. Churches are good for prayer, but so are garages and cars and mountains and showers and dance floors. Years ago I wrote an essay that began, "Some people think that God is in the details, but I have come to believe that God is in the bathroom." Prayer usually means praise, or surrender, acknowledging that you have run out of bullets. But there are no firm rules. As Rumi wrote, "There are hundreds of ways to kneel and kiss the ground." I just talk to God. I pray when people I love are sick, and I prayed when I didn't know whether I should have a baby. I pray when my work is horrible, or suddenly, miraculously, better. I cried out silently every few hours during the last two years of my mother's life. I even asked for help in coping with George W. Bush. I prayed that he would make decisions for the common good, which he has not done, but I pray that he might slip up and do it anyway. I do not pray for his success, as I do not pray for mine. I pray that he and his people do not destroy everything on the way down.

When I am in my right mind, which is about twice a month, I pray kindly.

Sam prayed for his dad every night.

Nothing happened. I determined to take this up with God when we meet: *Would it have been so much skin off your nose to give my child an answer?* I couldn't believe it. Usually if you pray from the heart, you get an answer— the phone rings or the mail comes, and light gets in through the cracks, so you can see the next right thing to do. That's all you need. But nothing happened at first. I secretly believed we'd bump into John at the market, per- haps, or at the movies, but we didn't. I kept calling the best friend, but it turned out I had the wrong number. Finally I found the right number, but the friend didn't know where John was, except that John's dad had been sick, so John was probably in town taking care of him. I called John's father again. No one answered.

Things got worse. I decided it would have been better if we'd never even tried. Sam had been doing fine before we'd started looking. Now he was frustrated, mad at his dad and more so at me. He said that if I were a better person, I would not have driven his father away. I wanted to find John, for Sam, but at the same time, I hadn't seen him in more than seven years, and I had, at best, mixed feelings about him. It was a mess. We got more frustrated, more stuck, less hopeful. Wendell Berry once said, at a coffeehouse in Mill Valley on a dark, rainy December day, "It gets darker and darker, and then Jesus is born." That line came back to me, from out of nowhere, and I decided to practice radical hope, hope in the face of not having a clue. I decided that God was not off doing the dishes while Sam sought help: God heard his prayers, and was working on it.

And within a week, the local paper carried John's father's obituary. This is God's own truth. The story said that Sam's grandfather had been cared for until the end by his only son. Sam's father was in town. I felt like a cartoon character who is standing too close to a huge Buddhist gong.

"I think I know where he is," I told Sam after school that day. "He's at his father's home." We decided to let a little time pass, so John could heal from the loss, and then Sam would write him a letter.

His letter began, "Hi, Dad, it's me, Sam, and I am a good boy."

He said he wanted to know him and to be friends. He put the letter in a small red box, with his favorite action figurines and some candy, and we took it to the post office.

A week later Sam heard from his father, who said he couldn't wait to meet him.

This is the only part of the story I am allowed to tell, except to say that a week after their first, shy meeting, a few days after their first meal together, John was standing in the doorway of Sam's second-grade classroom when school ended for the day. He was holding a soccer ball. Sam reported later that all the kids turned to look at him, having been prepared by Sam's teacher for the introduction, but one kid said anyway, "Who's that guy over there?"

And Sam said, "Oh—that's my dad."

Things are not perfect, because life is not TV and we are real people with scarred, worried hearts. But it's amazing a lot of the time. Where there was darkness, silence, and blame, there's now a family, and that means there's mess and misunderstanding, hurt feelings, and sighs. But it is a family: Sam and his father love and like each other. Can you imagine how impossible a dream this was for Sam? He even gets to whine about our shortcomings, like any old kid. For instance, on our first winter visit with John, the three of us making snow animals in a busy park, Sam said: "Why doesn't this family ever bring thermoses of cocoa, like other families?"

Things go wrong every time we visit, yet more things go well. Since we visit at Thanksgiving, it is always cold, and we are lit mostly by domestic fires, logs in the fireplace, candles. One year John took us to a frozen lake on a mountain, which you got to by gondola, where you could rent ice skates and buy hot food. John and I watched Sam skate. We got to be really proud at the same time. Maybe married parents always do this and it is not that big a deal. But it was to us. When we got too cold, we warmed ourselves over trashcans at the edge of the rink, in which people had built hobo fires with paper cups and wrappers and twigs they had found in the snow.

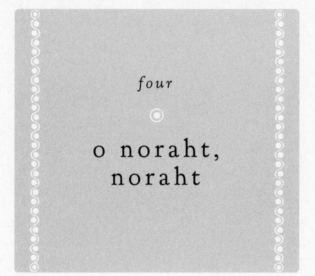

four

o noraht,
noraht

In a superhuman show of spiritual maturity, I moved my mother's ashes today from the back of the closet, where I'd shoved them a few weeks after she died. I was going to put them on the bookshelf, next to the three small pine boxes that held the pebbly ashes of our pets, now reincarnated as percussion instruments. My mother's ashes, by contrast, were returned in a brown plastic box, sealed, with her name spelled wrong: Dorothy Noraht Wyles Lamott; her middle name was Norah, not Noraht. She hated the name Norah, which I love, and she didn't go by Dorothy, which she also hated. She was called

"Nikki," the name of a character on a radio show that she had loved as a child in Liverpool.

I put the brown plastic box in the closet as soon as it came back from the funeral home, two years ago, thinking I could at *last* give up all hope that a wafting white-robed figure would rise from the ashes of my despair and say, "Oh, little one, my darling daughter, I am here for you now." I prayed for my heart to soften, to forgive her, and love her for what she did give me—life, great values, a lot of tennis lessons, and the best she could do. Unfortunately, the best she could do was terrible, like the Minister of Silly Walks trying to raise an extremely sensitive young girl, and my heart remained hardened toward her.

So I left her in the closet for two years to stew in her own ashes, and I refused to be nice to her, and didn't forgive her for being a terrified, furious, clinging, sucking maw of need and arrogance. I suppose that sounds harsh. I assumed Jesus wanted me to forgive her, but I also know he loves honesty and transparency. I don't think he was rolling his eyes impatiently at me while she was in the closet. I don't think much surprises him: this is how we make important changes—barely, poorly, slowly. And still, he raises his fist in triumph.

I've spent my whole life trying to get over having had Nikki for a mother, and I have to say that from day one after she died, I liked having a dead mother much more than having an impossible one. I began to call her Noraht as her *nom de mort*. I prayed to forgive her but didn't— for staying in a fever dream of a marriage, for fanatically pushing her children to achieve, for letting herself go from great beauty to hugely overweight woman in dowdy clothes and gloppy mask of makeup. It wasn't black and white: I really loved her, and took great care of her, and was proud of some heroic things she had done with her life. She had put herself through law school, fought the great good fights for justice and civil rights, marched against the war in Vietnam. But she was like someone who had broken my leg, and my leg had healed badly, and I would limp forever.

I couldn't pretend she hadn't done extensive damage— that's called denial. But I wanted to dance anyway, even with a limp. I know forgiveness is a component of free-dom, yet I couldn't, even after she died, grant her amnesty. Forgiveness means it finally becomes unimportant that you hit back. You're done. It doesn't necessarily mean that you want to have lunch with the person. If you keep hitting back, you stay trapped in the nightmare—which is the tiny problem with our Israeli and Palestinian friends. And I guess I wasn't done.

I stored her in the closet, beside her navy blue purse, which the nurses had given me when I checked her into a convalescent home nearby, three months before she died. I'd go pick up the ashes from time to time, and say to them, grimly, "Hello, Noraht." Then I'd put them back. My life has been much better since she died, and it was liberating to be so angry, after having been such a good and loyal girl. But eighteen months after her death, I still thought of her the same way I do about George Bush—with bewilderment that this person could ever be in charge, and dismay, and something like hatred. I decided to see whether I could find some flecks of light. Friends told me to pray, and to go slowly, because otherwise, with my rage so huge, how would I be able to see fireflies in the flames? I should try to go as safely, and as deeply, as I could into the mystery of our relationship. I couldn't scatter the ashes—the box was sealed. So I went through my mother's purse.

It looked like a doctor's bag, worn and dusty, with two handles, the sort of purse Ruth Buzzi, of *Laugh-In* fame, might hit you with. I opened it, and began pulling out

Kleenex like a magician pulling endless scarves from his sleeve. This was very distressing. My mother's Kleenex had been distressing to me my whole life. They always smelled like the worst of her, all her efforts to disguise herself—the makeup, the perfume and lotion and lipstick and powder, all gone rancid. And she'd swab you with Kleenex to clean you up, with her spit. It was disgusting. In her last years, she fumbled for them, and finding them, not remember why she'd needed them. My mother almost never cried—her parents were English—so the Kleenex weren't to wipe her tears; and she had drowned in those uncried tears.

Uncried-tears syndrome left my mother hypervigilant, unable to settle down into herself, and—to use the clinical term—cuckoo.

Her purse was a weight, ballast; it tethered her to the earth as her mind floated away. It was also health and preparedness, filled with anything you might need. For instance, there were a lot of Band-Aids. You never know when you'll need one, only that in this world, you will. There were pads of Post-its; they gave her confidence that she could keep track of things, if only she could remember to write things down and stick the Post-its somewhere. And then remember to look at them.

There were house keys, which made me feel such grief that I had taken away her freedom. But my mother had an unbelievable life for someone so sick with Alzheimer's and Type II diabetes, and so poor, for as long as my brothers and I could pull it off. We helped her have independence and a great view, and her cat, and her friends, until the very end. When we put her in the home, her freedom was gone anyway. She had only the freedom, when the nurse left at night, to fall when she tried to get up to pee; to lie in wet sheets; to get stuck on the balcony and not remember how to get back in.

There were mirrors in her purse, so she could see that she was still there: Am I still here? Peekaboo! There I am. There were a dozen receipts from Safeway, which was right across the street from her retirement community. She was supposed to be on a strict low-carbohydrate diet to help control her diabetes, but every single receipt was for bread and cookies, which she'd sneak out to buy when the nurses or I were off doing the laundry. I kind of like that in a girl. She also bought dozens of tubes of Crystal Light, intensely flavored diet drink flakes you mix with water. She must have hoped they'd fly straight into her brain, like Pop Rocks, and energize it like Tinkerbell.

There were a number of receipts from our HMO in her purse, handed to her over time; she had been told to hold on to them until she was called, and so she did, because she was a good girl. She loved the nurses, and she loved her doctor, so the receipts were like love letters she'd never throw away. She had a card with the direct line of a nurse who helped her clip her terrible rhino toe-nails. People always gave her special things, like their direct lines, because she was so eager and dignified and needy, and everyone wanted to reward and help her. People lined up to wait on her, to serve her, her whole life.

There was also a large, heavy tube of toothpaste in the purse. Maybe she had bought it one day at Safeway, and never remembered to take it out. Maybe she liked people to sneak peeks of it in her purse: it said of her, I may be lost, but my breath is fresh, or could be. There were three travel-size containers of hand lotion, a lipstick, a compact, and six cards from cab companies—Safe, Friendly, Professional. Just what you need in this world. She could always get home when she got lost, which she did, increasingly.

I kept putting off opening her wallet. There would be pictures inside. Finally I opened it, and found it filled with cards. She had library cards from thirty years ago, membership cards for the Democratic Party and the ACLU and the Sierra Club. There were two credit cards, which had expired before her mind did. She had an insane, destructive relationship to money, like a junkie. There was never enough, so she charged things, charged away a whole life, to pump herself out of discomfort and fear. She assault-shopped.

There were photos of my nephew Tyler, my older brother's son, and of Sam. She loved being a grandmother. And there was an old picture of herself, a black-and-white photo from when she was twenty-one or so. She was a beautiful woman, who looked a little like Theda Bara, white face, jet-black hair. She had dark eyes, full of unflinching intelligence and depression and eagerness to please. In this photo, she looked as if she was trying to will herself into elegance, whereas her life was always hard and messy and full of scrabbling chaos. Her frog-stretched mouth was trying to smile, but she couldn't, or maybe wouldn't, because then she would look beautiful and triumphant, and there would be no rescue, no one to help or serve or save her.

She'd kept all of her cards from the years she spent practicing family law in Hawaii—a state bar association card, and her driver's license, which expired in 1985. In the license photo, she was brown from the Hawaiian sun, soft and rosy, as if she had risen through warm water, but her eyes were afraid, as though she might have been about to sink to the bottom again. And she did, and clung to our necks to save her.

Her purse said, "I'm a liberal, and a grandmother, and I keep my teeth clean and my skin soft. If I can't remember something, I can write it down. If I get a cut, I'll bandage it right away." Her purse made my heart ache. I threw away most of the contents that day—the Kleenex, the lotions, the toothpaste—and the purse itself. It was a dusty navy blue organ she didn't need anymore. I kept her wallet and the things in it, even the old library cards. I glanced in a small mirror she carried. It scares me how alike we look. I wear glasses now, as she did. I look tired—I am tired. And I have a pouch below my belly, whereas I had a thin waist before. Now there's this situation down there, low and grabbable. If it had a zipper, you could store stuff in it, as in a fanny pack.

I put the wallet back in the closet, next to my mother's ashes. I said a prayer, to Jesus: "Here. Could you watch her a while longer?" I left her ashes there for another six months. It was during that time that my three pets died. I was inconsolable. You want a great mother, I'll show you a Labrador-retriever mix. Yet there was great happiness, too, because I fell in love. I went to Hawaii with my boyfriend but got very worried beforehand about how I'd look in a swimsuit. My friend Robyn suggested that I rub lotion lovingly into my thighs, so they would feel cared for, and that I decorate them with small flower tattoos. It helped, and while I did not quite look like Brigitte Bardot in her heyday, I felt better, and this, on a beach, can be a miracle.

I had that on my mind when I got up this morning, for no particular reason—the lotion, and the rose tattoos. After breakfast, I went and got the brown plastic box of ashes out of the closet. I couldn't very well rub lotion into it, but I sat with it in my lap. The pouch on my belly is nice for holding children, so I let my mother sit there for a few minutes. Then I wrapped the box in birthday gift paper, lavender and blue with silver stars, and taped a picture of a red rose on it. I got a little carried away—hey, late Happy Birthday, Noraht—because the thing is, I don't actually forgive her much yet. Besides, only part of a day had passed, and I was definitely not hating her anymore. Grace means you're in a different universe from where you had been stuck, when you had absolutely no way to get there on your own.

When it happens—when you stop hating—you have to pinch yourself. Jesus said, "The point is to not hate and kill each other today, and if you can, to help the forgotten and powerless. Can you write that down, and leave it by the phone?" So I picked up my mother's ashes, and put them on a shelf in the living room, and stood beside them for a while.

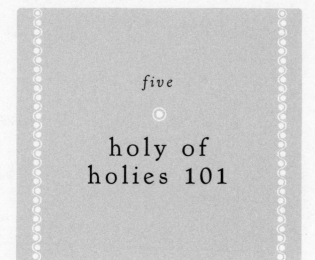

five

holy of
holies 101

I did not mean to help start a Sunday school, and did not have a speck of confidence that I could do so: I have only mediocre self-esteem when I am doing things that I am good at or that don't require any self-esteem. I grow anxious on my way to the dump with a car full of garbage, convinced that my garbage and I will be rejected, either because I am throwing out perfectly good stuff, or because it is so disgusting that the people who run the dump wouldn't want it. I suffer from what a psychiatrist friend calls clinical sensitivity; she recommends that I avoid too much stimulation. I do not particularly like large groups of children, which is to say, more than two at a time, and I could not bear to miss any of the regular service, with which Sunday school would be concurrent. There was one more problem: There weren't any children, except Sam.

But six years ago I came to believe that I was supposed to start a Sunday school, while our church was temporarily located at a senior center during the construction of a new building. The land that our old building was on was part of a redevelopment plan for Marin City. Our building was falling to pieces. I like this in a church. You see more clearly how held together we are, in spite of the sags and the creakiness and the buckled floors. Gravity is still in effect. And besides, down the street, the builders were including classrooms in the new church building.

One day at the senior center, I could feel something tugging on my inside sleeve, which is the only place I ever hear from God: on the shirtsleeve of my heart. I understood that someone needed to start a school, because it was the right thing to do, and most important, I needed to make church more fun for Sam.

I was utterly open to the call, in a tense, clinically sensitive way. So I told Kris, my best friend at St. Andrew, that we were having a call.

"We are?" she asked.

I nodded grimly.

"Where would we start?"

I know that with writing, you start where you are, and you flail around for a while, and if you keep doing it, every day you get closer to something good. Carolyn Myss said that we are responsible not for the outcome of things, but only for the ingredients, so Kris and I bought everything we could think of that young children would need to learn about God: juice boxes, blankets, beach balls, moist towelettes, a children's Bible, a boom box, and art supplies.

"And what will we teach them?" Kris asked.

This was a problem. I don't know much about God; only that He or She is love, and is not American, or male. I do love Jesus, and I'm nuts about his mother. Mary Oliver said something to the effect that the best sermon she ever heard was the sun. I thought, That's the sort of thing we'll teach.

You're not supposed to love Mary so much, if you're not Catholic, but I do. I wear a picture of her inside a gold oval frame, on a thin gold chain. Her arms outstretched in blessing look as if she has pulled the orange lining out of her blue robes to show everyone that there's nothing hidden inside, no tricks up her sleeves. Golden light pours forth from the pocket linings as if, were she to put her hands back in her pockets, the light would be plugged up from inside. "She looks so cas," Sam said once—for "casual." She doesn't look like she has missed many meals, either, not the usual anorexic piety. She looks like Myrna Loy.

I wear Mary for two reasons: Because she helps me remember the song "Let It Be." And because I used to pray to her as if she were my mother when I was coming down off cocaine. I'd lie in bed beside whatever cute coked-out boyfriend I had at the time, who'd be snoring and muttering while I ground my teeth in the dark.

Hail Mary, full of grace. This is what the angel says before telling Mary that she will be Jesus' mother. Denise Levertov writes:

> She did not cry, "I cannot, I am not worthy,"
> Nor, "I have not the strength."
> She did not submit with gritted teeth,
>
> > raging, coerced.
>
> Bravest of all humans,
>
> > consent illumined her.

This is so, so not me.

When I used to lie in the dark grinding my teeth, utterly whipped, surrender came, and then the miracle, motherly kindness toward my own screwed-up self. One reason you're not supposed to be a big Mary enthusiast if you are Protestant is that you might be overcome with the need to genuflect in public places. But Mary is for me the feminine face of divine love. Archbishop Carlo Maria Martini of Milan wrote that "full of grace" is in the passive: grace is something Mary has received, and the phrase is in the distant past tense, so it really means something like, "You have been loved for a very long time." Knowing this—that I could call on a woman who had been loved for so long, stretching backward and forward through millennia—could trump my self-loathing, and I would hail Mary even as I imagined hitting the man next to me over the head with my tennis racket.

I have been hailing her all along, through my son's birth and early childhood, right through to these teenage years, through all the men I've been with, through my son's reunion with his father, through health scares, through my mother's terrible death of Alzheimer's, through the early days of my love affair with the man I've been with for a while now. But some of the most desperate hailing I've done has been in the years of trying to help start a Sunday school at St. Andrew Presbyterian.

◉

We moved out of the senior center into our new church, which had a nursery and two classrooms. Word got out in the community that a new Sunday school had started at St. Andrew, and children started arriving. Soon we had eleven kids: four black, four white, two Mexican, and one Asian—reflecting the make-up of the church. Each week I announced in church that I would take the children after the children's sermon, and that we would be needing adult volunteers. We took the children to a classroom, gave them each a juice box and some corn chips, and tried to teach them about God's love—about the beauty that enlivens our hearts, that awakens and welcomes us, even in our current conditions. Usually, at the end of the hour, one child had been in tears. But Sam started to bring his friends.

It turned out that I did not like children, or at any rate, they made me extremely nervous, and I had almost nothing to share with them, except that Jesus loved them, and I did, too, even when I was in a bad mood. I had imagined a wacky sort of rainbow love fest. I had not counted on so many minor injuries. For example, I had hoped we could throw around a beach ball while we memorized a line of Scripture—calling out one sentence, like "Come unto me, all ye who are weary and heavy-laden, and I will give you rest." But the kids had the attention spans of fruit bats, and the boys would throw the ball too hard at one another, as if playing dodge ball. I quickly switched to "God is love," but the children could barely remember that, either, and wanted it to be their turn only so they could try to hurt the others with the beach ball. "God is love," I said through clenched teeth, and then threw the ball to a girl, who froze, so that it slapped her in the face like a whale's tale.

Finally, three adults came to help, all middle-aged white women. This was sort of frustrating, but one of the immutable laws of being human is that the people who show up are the right people. We met every few weeks. We figured out that the only things that worked were a short Bible story, the juice boxes, and art, and so we stuck with those.

The teachers were all hard-core left-wing types, and that worked for me. One secret of life is that the reason life works at all is that not everyone in your tribe is nuts

on the same day. Another secret is that laughter is car-
bonated holiness.

I clutched my Mary medallion when things went
south, which was often. When I clutched it, I could hear
the Beatles singing "Let It Be," over the sound of the
voices in my head. The mean voice in my head said that
this was a catastrophe, white liberal guilt run amok, a
total waste of time—day care, not church school. The
mean voice said that when you don't have a clue what's
going on, maybe it's better that you not be in charge of a
lot of things, which is something I keep meaning to point
out to George Bush. But the kind voice said, So what if it's
day care—it's enough to be there for the children. And
they liked it.

During the Cuban Missile Crisis, President Kennedy
received two letters from the Kremlin. One was aggres-
sive, the other gentler. And because Kennedy said to his
men, "Let's respond to the saner message," we didn't get
blown up, or have to blow up the world. So I tried to
respond to the kinder voice.

Some days went better than others. Most of the time, I
could relate to the kids, all of them—black, white, rich,
poor, in between—and to the stress and loneliness of their

lives. I nearly broke under the weight of these myself, as far back as I can remember. I think that by kindergarten, the only thing that could have helped me was a nice refreshing drink. If you had just given me a flask, I could have handled things a lot better.

One Sunday when there were too many kids, and not enough teachers, we decided to write cards to people who were reviled in the world. This had been the Bible study: If you want to feel close to Jesus, find the people who are suffering, or whom the world doesn't value. The kids made cards for kids in juvenile hall, and Israel, and Palestine; one boy made a card for George Bush. And two seven-year-old girls came up to me and asked, "What was the name of the woman whose two dogs killed the teacher last year?"

"Marjorie Knoller?" I asked, astounded.

They made a card for Marjorie with cats and suns and glitter blobs, which said, "We are from St. Andrew and we are saying hello because we know you did not want your dogs to kill that girl."

People from church made sandwiches for us every week, peanut butter and jelly on whole wheat, and brought bags of Doritos, and fruit, and prayed for us. We got by. But it was hard. Some of the kids were needy and vulnerable and depressed, with faces of dubious, aged concern, rumpled foreheads, downcast or shuttered eyes. Some were wild. We did not exclude anyone, because Jesus didn't.

On bad days, I could not imagine what he had been thinking.

I could always feel Jesus in the room, encouraging us in every way, although maybe he would have stopped short of sharing Doritos with us. But peanut butter and jelly on whole wheat, definitely, and juice boxes when it was hot.

Holiness has most often been revealed to me in the exquisite pun of the first syllable, in holes—in not enough help, in brokenness, mess. High holy places, with ethereal sounds and stained glass, can massage my illusion of holiness, but in holes and lostness I can pick up the light of small ordinary progress, newly made moments flecked like pepper into the slog and the disruptions.

When we did art with the kids, the demons would lie down.

Other times, I would be so angry with the kids that I would get a stomachache from the effort of suppressing my anger, and I would watch the clock, trying to wear down the morning. Someone long ago said that God is not a boss or a judge, that God is a purpose, and I tried to live by this. My purpose was to show up and offer myself to people who were having a hard time, and part of doing that was to run this funky school.

We kept lurching forward. It reminded me of driving through the rain to do an errand in the rural parts of Marin, on the road that leads to the ocean, past farmland and forest: you drive worriedly through poor visibility on a slippery surface, and you think you're heading to one place, for a certain efficient reason, but you space out for a while, and there's slippage in the sky, and all at once a long, low beam of sun slants through.

For a while at Sunday school there was a girl who seemed retarded; she rarely spoke. She was so black her skin looked navy blue, and she had a huge growth on one eyelid. What did we have to offer her? Juice boxes, decent art supplies, and our beliefs that love and patience would be like Holiness Helper in her life.

The girl appeared to be very sad much of the time, but she loved to draw. One difficult day, I let her sit in my lap next to the open window, while the other teacher read the children their Bible story. She studied the dust in the air while we listened, and kept putting her finger out, like

E.T., to touch the glitter. The dust was letting her see the air, suspended as we are, held and blown about, even though we appear to be sitting, planted. The dust made the invisible visible, for a few moments, immersing both of us in another dimension, beyond what we could usually see.

Even as we improved as teachers and as students, the children continued to have raging impulse-control problems; the very thing that made them spontaneous and immediate could also make them mean. One day, a mouthy eight-year-old said something insulting about my dreadlocks. Rather than hit him over the head with the Wiffle Ball bat, which was my first impulse, I sat beside him and said, "It's only been in the last ten years that I learned how beautiful my hair and I are, so please don't say critical things about me. It hurts my feelings."

He gaped at me, and said, "You're freaking me out, Octopus Head."

The other teachers and I had dreamed of taking the kids on field trips, to remove them from the grip and tangle of life—of a day on the beach; of sandy, sacramental hot dogs; of playing in the ocean, making sculptures, and drawing with sticks. But we could barely manage them in class.

Then there was the fact that although there were equal numbers of blacks and whites in the church, all the teachers were white. We wanted the influence of the black adults. But only a few of them volunteered to assist (we gratefully put them on the schedule), and we white teachers were too shy to say anything. Even at a progressive and diverse church like ours, it's sometimes hard to bring up uncomfortable racial issues. After a while, though, there was a small breakthrough.

One of our teachers, a blue-eyed blonde, stepped to the pulpit during worship to talk about something that was tearing her up. She was teaching Sunday school that day, and had to make it quick. She said that even though she was a progressive and a civil rights activist, she had secret thoughts about race that scared her, that made her feel she did not deserve to be part of the church anymore. She'd been watching the news, she told us, and the image of a black man in a T-shirt had flashed on the TV screen, and her first thought had been, "What did he do?" He hadn't done anything—he was an expert on the law. She didn't have a clue where to begin with this old ugly thing inside her, except to stand before us, crying, and say it.

Then she walked down the aisle to go teach, and so she did not see that every single person in the church had stood to applaud her.

While she had not been referring specifically to her confusion about the lack of adults of color at the Sunday school, her words wedged open the topic of race. We let things sit for a while before being more specific, because somehow, without our particularly noting it, we had grown to enjoy Sunday school more and thus were not as resentful that only white people were teaching. Time and one another's support had helped us develop muscles—as when Sam helped me start doing push-ups. At first, it was pathetic. But he bossed me until I could manage six or seven, and eventually three sets of ten.

I protested: "Jesus never forced Mary to do push-ups."

"Mary was a weakling."

But Mary was anything but weak. Denise Levertov writes:

But we are told of meek obedience. No one mentions courage.

    The engendering Spirit
did not enter her without consent.

I know what Sam meant, though. He meant bony, and worried, like the Mary in most art. I personally like to think she looked like a demure Bette Midler.

We read the kids Scripture every week, even though they squirmed and yawned—we had concluded that people who made farting noises, and weapons out of Doritos, should not determine what we did and didn't do in class. There's a lovely Hasidic story of a rabbi who always told his people that if they studied the Torah, it would put Scripture on their hearts. One of them asked, "Why *on* our hearts, and not *in* them?" The rabbi answered, "Only God can put Scripture inside. But reading sacred text can put it on your hearts, and then when your hearts break, the holy words will fall inside."

We often had a dozen six- to nine-year-olds, and another dozen ten- to twelve-year-olds, with five or six babies and toddlers careening around. We thought of a youth group for our teenagers, but we didn't have enough staff. Actually, we didn't have any teenagers, either, but would soon. Sam was twelve and a half, as were two other kids. We needed more people to help. We kept talking to one another, and to our pastor, Veronica, and then were ready to talk to the congregation. A few of us came to the pulpit. We said that we believed that the truth would set us free, and the truth was that the Sunday-school staff was burned out, that there were almost no people of color, and that if we didn't get more help, we'd have to close down.

The shit hit the fan, to use the theological expression.

A number of people in the church were outraged, both parents and nonparents; they felt they had been ambushed and judged. Others, of every race, came forward to support us, although they did not offer to help teach. I heard that people were talking behind our backs, and I wanted to call Veronica and tell on them—Pastor, Pastor, so-and-so was bearing false witness against us! I felt shame, and a hopelessness that there could ever be, even in one church, let alone the nation, true racial reconciliation.

I nursed my resentments and disgrace like young plants, watering them, trimming back the dead leaves, making sure they got enough sunlight.

At times like these, I believe, Jesus rolls up his sleeves, smiles roguishly, and thinks, "This is good." He lets me get nice and crazy, until I can't take my own thinking and solutions for one more moment. The next morning, I got on my knees and prayed, "Please, please help me. Please let me feel You while I adjust to not getting what I was hoping for." And then I remembered Rule 1: When all else fails, follow instructions. And Rule 2: Don't be an asshole.

I called the person with whom I was angriest, and I apologized for harboring resentment toward her. She said, "I'm so glad you called. That was brave of you." I tugged at my Mary.

It was one of those tortured, blame-filled, wounded conversations I associate with old boyfriends, where they get to come across as very calm and centered, while I sound ten minutes away from being institutionalized. The woman listened to my frustration that the Sunday-school teachers were exhausted. Then I cried from the heart, "Why don't more of you black people help us with the kids?"

She did not say anything, in an extremely loud way.

"That's not what I meant." I started to fume. "It came out wrong." But in the sickening silence of held breath, I realized that that was indeed what I'd meant to say.

"Annie," she said, very kindly. She asked me if it was possible that the only people who felt they had a skill or calling to teach all happened to be white.

I didn't know about that. I think we both wanted to get off the phone, but we stuck it out; and we simply kept talking. By the time we hung up, things weren't quite as strained between us. I sat on the couch, astonished. God must see me as so many people at once: beloved, nuts, luminous, full of shadow.

Then I called everyone else I was mad at.

Some conversations went better than others, but not one person volunteered to help. Yet time, and showing up, turn most messes to compost, and something surprising may grow, and I have noticed this especially at my church. Over the next weeks, half a dozen people committed to helping once a month—black, white, men and women—and a young Asian man agreed to teach the Gospel through martial arts. Now we have a dozen adults, a paid director, and as many as thirty kids, a youth group of six or seven, and several little ones.

The youth group is close-knit, integrated, and fierce in maintaining its boundaries. You must be thirteen or older to belong, no exceptions. I tried to bribe Sam into letting my friend Pammy's twelve-year-old daughter come one Sunday, and he shook his head, unrelenting.

The other teachers and I took the teenagers out for a day at the ocean not long ago. Stinson Beach was blue and

breezy, and the kids stood looking around like develop-
ers. After a while, the roar of the ocean, the smells, the
hard sand here and the soft sand there, the sun on their
faces and the frigid water on their feet, changed them:
they started to move, and to throw stuff at one another. I
grew up on the beaches of West Marin, taking in the presents the ocean gives, plastic made beautiful, glass turned
to jewels, calligraphy on the sand—bird tracks, foot-
prints, seaweed—and you couldn't get us kids out of the
water until we were blue and shivering. I stood on the
beach that day with our youth group, hailing Mary; then I
got up my courage and waded in, to my knees. The ocean
is so female, amniotic, and the waves and sand scour you
like a mother with a washcloth.

The kids went in. They yelped as the cold water covered them, and they splashed and screamed, and shoved
one another a little more roughly than they had in my
dream of this day. Still, as I watched them being cuffed
by the breaking waves, submerged, missing for a moment,
then reappearing, spluttering, laughing, I thought of what
this dream had taken: all those times we teachers had had
to ask for help, and had plugged away without enough
resources, without knowing how, or whether, we were
going to manage. And it had taken much more letting go

and trusting than we had felt capable of. I remember getting knocked around in these waves when I was young, and how it felt when grown-ups picked you up and tossed you into the air or the water, exciting and scary all at once, and you knew you would always be caught.

six

this dog's life

Having a good dog is the closest some of us will ever come to knowing the direct love of a mother, or God, so it's no wonder it knocked the stuffing out of Sam and me when Sadie died. I promised Sam we'd get another puppy someday, but privately I resolved to never get another dog. I didn't want to hurt that much again, if I could possibly avoid it. And I didn't want my child's heart and life to break like that again. But you don't always get what you want; you get what you get. This is a real problem for me. You want to protect your child from pain, and what you get instead is life, and grace; and though theologians insist that grace is freely given, the truth is that sometimes you pay for it through the nose. And you can't pay your child's way.

We should never have gotten a dog to begin with—they all die. While it is subversive when artists make art that will pass away in the fullness of time, or later that day, it's not as ennobling when your heart breaks.

When Sam was two, and George Herbert Walker Bush was president, I noticed I was depressed and afraid a lot of the time. I figured that I needed to move, to marry an armed man, or to find a violent but well-behaved dog. I was determined, as I am now, to stay and fight, and the men I tended to love were not remotely well enough to carry guns, so I was stuck with the dog idea.

For a while I called people who were advertising dogs in the local paper. All of them said they had the perfect dog, but perfect for whom? Quentin Tarantino? One dog we auditioned belonged to a woman who said the dog adored children, but it lunged at Sam, snarling. Other dogs snapped at us. One ran to hide, peeing as she ran. I took the initiative and placed an ad for a mellow, low-energy guard dog, and soon got a call from a woman who said she had just the dog.

As it turned out, she did have a great dog, a gorgeous two-year-old named Sadie, half black Lab, half golden retriever. Sadie looked like a black Irish setter. I always told people she was like Jesus in a black fur coat, or Audrey Hepburn in Blackglama, elegant and loving and silly. Such a lady.

Sadie was shy at first. The vet said she might have been abused as a puppy, because she acted worried about not pleasing us. He taught us how to get on the floor with her and plow into her slowly, so that she would see that we meant her no harm—that we were, in fact, playing with her. She tried to look nonchalant, but you could see she was alarmed. She was so eager to please, though, that she learned to play, politely.

Sadie lived with us for more than ten years, and saw us through great joy and great losses. She consoled us through friends' illnesses, through the deaths of Sam's grandparents. She and I walked Sam to school every day. She was mother, dad, psych nurse. She helped me survive my boyfriends and the sometimes metallic, percussive loneliness in between them. She helped Sam survive his first mean girlfriend. She'd let my mother stroke her head forever. She taught comfort.

But when she was about to turn thirteen, she developed lymphoma. The nodes in her neck were the size of golf balls. The vet said she would live a month if we didn't treat her. Part of me wanted to let her die, so we could get it over with, have the pain behind us. But Sam and I talked it over, and decided she would have half a dose of chemo: we wanted her to have one more good spring. She was better two days after the chemo. She must have had a great capacity for healing: she went in and out of remission for two years. Toward the end, when she got sick again and probably wasn't going to get well, the vet said he would walk us through her death. He said that even when a being is extremely sick, ninety-five percent of that being is still healthy and well—it's just that the other five percent feels so shitty. We should focus on the parts that were well, he said, the parts that brought her pleasure, like walks, being stroked, smelling things, and us.

Our vet does not like to put animals to sleep unless they are suffering, and Sadie did not seem to be in pain. He said that one day she would go under a bed and not come out, and when she did, he would give us sedatives to help her stay calm. One day she crawled under my bed, just as he said she would.

It was a cool, dark cave under my bed, with a soft moss-green carpet. Sadie's breathing was labored. She looked apologetic.

I called the vet and asked if I should bring her in. He said she'd feel safer dying at home, with me, but I should come in to pick up the narcotics. He gave me three syringes full. I took them under the bed with me, along with the telephone, with the ringer off, and I thought about injecting them all into my arm so my heart would not hurt so much. I wonder whether this would be considered a relapse by the more rigid members of the recovery community. I lay beside Sadie and assured her that she was a good dog even though she could no longer take care of us. I prayed for her to die quickly and without pain, for her sake, but mostly because I wanted her to die before Sam got home from school. I didn't want him to see her dead body. She hung on. I gave her morphine, prayed, talked to her softly, and called the vet. He had me put the phone beside her head, and listened for a moment.

"She's really not in distress," he assured me. "This is hard work, like labor. And she has you, Jesus, and narcotics. We should all be so lucky."

I stayed beside her on the carpet under the bed. At one point Sadie raised her head to gaze around, looking like a black horse. Then she sighed, laid her head down, and died.

I couldn't believe that she was gone, even though she'd been sick for so long. I could feel that something huge, a tide, had washed in, and then washed out.

I cried and cried, and called my brother and sister-in-law. Jamie said Stevo wasn't home, but she would leave him a note and come right over. I prayed again, for my brother to be there before Sam came home from school, so he could take Sadie's body away, to spare Sam, to spare me from Sam's loss.

I kept looking at the clock. School would be out in half an hour.

Jamie and their dog, Sasha, arrived seventeen minutes after Sadie died. I had pulled the carpet out from under the bed. Sadie looked as beautiful as ever. Jamie and I sat on the floor nearby. Sasha is a small white dog with tea-colored stains; she has perky ears and tender eyes and a bright, dancing quality—we call her the Czechoslovakian circus terrier—and we couldn't resist her charm. She licked us and ran up to Sadie and licked her, too, on her face. Then she ran back to us, as if to say, "I am life, and I am here! And my ears are up at this hilarious angle!"

Stevo finally arrived, only a few minutes before Sam was usually home from school. I wanted my brother to hurry and put Sadie in the car, but it was too horrible to think that Sam might catch him sneaking Sadie out like a burglar stealing our TV. So I breathed miserably, and prayed to be up to the task. Stevo sat beside Jamie. Then Sam arrived home and found us. He cried out sharply and sat on my bed alone, above Sadie. His eyes were red, but after a while Sasha made him laugh. She kept running over to the dead, exquisitely boneless mountain of majestic glossy black dog in repose on the rug. And she leaped on the bed to kiss Sam, before tending to the rest of us, like a doctor making her rounds.

Soon things got wild: My friend Neshama came over, and sat down beside me. I had called her with the news. Then a friend of Sam's stopped by, with his father, who slipped behind Sam on the bed like a shadow. The doorbell rang again, and it was another friend of Sam's, just passing by, out of the blue, if you believe in out of the blue, which I don't; and then a kid who lives up the hill came to borrow Sam's bike. He stayed, too. It was like the stateroom scene in *A Night at the Opera*. There were five adults, four kids, one white Czechoslovakian circus terrier, and one large dead black dog.

Sadie looked like an island of dog, and we looked like flotsam that had formed a ring around her. Life, death, dogs—something in us was trying to hold something together that doesn't hold together, but then does, miraculously, for the time being.

Sometimes we were self-consciously quiet, as if we were on the floor in kindergarten, and should stretch out and nap, but the teacher had gone out, and so we waited.

The boys eventually went downstairs and turned on loud rock 'n' roll. The grown-ups stayed a while longer. I got a bag of chocolates from the kitchen, and we ate them, as if raising a toast. As Sadie grew deader and emptier, we could see that it was no longer Sadie in there. She wasn't going to move or change, except to get worse and start smelling. So Stevo carried her on the rolled-up carpet out to my van. It was so clumsy, and so sweet, this ungainly car-size package, Sadie's barge, and sarcophagus.

We could hear the phantom sounds of Sadie for days—the nails on wood, the tail, the panting. Sam was alternately distant and clingy and mean, because I am the primary person he banks on and bangs on. I stayed close enough so he could push me away. Sadie slowly floated off.

Then, out of the so-called blue again, six months later, some friends gave us a five-month-old puppy, Lily. She's a Rottweiler/Shar-Pei/shepherd mix, huge, sweet, and well behaved—mostly. She's not a stunning bathing beauty like Sadie. But she's lovely and loving, and we adore her. It still hurts sometimes, to have lost Sadie, though. She was like the floating garlands the sculptor Andy Golds-worthy made in the documentary *Rivers and Tides*: yellow and red and green leaves, connected one to another with thorns, floating away in the current, swirling, drifting back toward the shore, getting cornered in eddies, drift-ing free again. All along you know that they will disperse once they're out of your vision, but they will never be gone entirely, because you saw them. The leaves show you how water is like the wind, because they do what stream-ers do in a breeze. The garlands are a translation of this material; autumn leaves, transposed to water, still flutter.

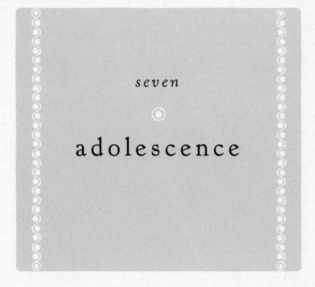

seven

adolescence

The day after Sam turned thirteen, we were going through our usual hormonal transformations together, which is to say, sometimes the house gets crowded. There was Sam at thirteen—usually mellow, funny, slightly nuts. But when the plates of the earth shifted, there was the Visitor, the Other. I called him Phil. Phil was tense. Also sullen and contemptuous. There was me at forty-eight—usually mellow, funny, and slightly nuts—and there was the Menopausal Death Crone.

Some days were great, because Sam and I at these ages were wild and hilarious and utterly full of our best stuff;

but other days, when Phil and the Death Crone dropped by, were awful. We sniggered impatiently, and sighed and gripped our foreheads, and we fought. We fought mostly about homework and church, neither of which works for Sam—but then again, neither does flossing. It's hard for him to sit still for school and church when he'd rather be hanging out with friends or playing at the computer, and I hate to make him sit still, because I want him to be happy and to find an authentic spirituality, and because his resistance pollutes my home and my worship.

The usual things helped: some distance, prayer, chocolate. Talking to the parents of older kids was helpful for me, since parents of kids the same age as yours won't admit how horrible their children are. There's a great book on adolescence that I can turn to, *Get out of My Life, but First Could You Drive Me and Cheryl to the Mall?* by Anthony Wolf. I taped things to the wall that give me some light to see by. One pink card says, "Breathe, Pray, Be kind, Stop grabbing." Another card says something I heard recently, that you can either practice being right or practice being kind. Screaming in the car helped.

But what helped most of all was walking. I had been going up on Mount Tamalpais to walk and be quiet and pray nearly every morning for years. I started to do this because I had heard that Jesus did so, although my friend Father Tom recently clarified this. He said that we are not sure whether Jesus actually did this; people had to explain Jesus' absence by saying he was going up to the mountain to pray, but for all we know, he went off and had a few beers. Then he may have gone bowling, slinging the ball bitterly down the alley until he felt better.

"What would he have done with thirteen-year-olds?" I asked Tom.

"In biblical times, they used to stone a few thirteen-year-olds with some regularity, which helped keep the others quiet and at home. The mothers were usually in the first row of stone throwers, and had to be restrained."

I wrote this down and taped it to my wall, next to the pink card. Every parent who saw it laughed and felt better; nothing helps like letting your ugly common secrets out. And it came in handy during a recent fight.

◉

I was driving Sam to his friend Anthony's house, where he was going to spend the night. I would pick him up for church at ten-thirty the next morning. He was furious about having to go to church, although he has to go only every other week. The Visitor, Phil, had been with us all morning, petulant and put-upon—what we called "bratty" when I was young. When I'd asked Sam to wash his breakfast dishes, you'd have thought I had ordered him to give the kitty a flea dip.

I didn't try to get him to want to come to church; I didn't try to bribe him, or get him to like it—or me. I am not here to be his friend. He was awful in the car, mute and victimized.

It was one of those long ten-minute car rides. Living with a teenager can feel like living with an ex, or with a drug addict who has three days clean and sober. I tried to think about how nice it would be not to see Sam for twenty-four hours. We both sighed a lot. When I pulled up at Anthony's house, Sam got out of the car, and without saying good-bye, slammed the door and walked away. And I blew up. This is one thing they forget to mention in most child-rearing books, that at times you will just lose your mind. Period.

So I lost it, and I shouted for him to come back and get in the car. He couldn't believe his ears. He gave me a withering look that turned to desperation. "No, no, please," he begged.

"Get in the car," I said. "You do *not* slam the door and walk away from me."

I made him get in the car and close the door, and I drove away. He was furious, then teary. He tried begging for mercy. I hate that.

I parked where the road dead-ended near Anthony's, and I got out. I said, "You will not treat me like shit. I'm going to sit by that log. When you're ready to apologize with a contrite heart, you can get out of the car."

I went and sat down against an ancient fallen log, and smoldered.

I did not look back at him, thirty feet away. I looked at the log instead. I caught my breath. I thought about what a piece of shit I am, and what a horrible, ruined child he is. I thought about grounding him all weekend, but of course, that meant I would have to spend time with him. I breathed, as it said on the pink card, and prayed, tried to be kind to my disastrous self, and wondered what it might mean in this situation to stop grabbing.

The log had a certain eminence, the majesty of age—there was rot, and hairy sprouts, the kind you see in a grandfather's ears. It was furniture, a barrier, sculptural and grave, not the sort of thing you could argue with.

I could feel Sam's eyes drilling into my head. I felt wrong, and wronged. My head was sticking up over the log, so he could have shot at me.

A few feet away was a rock that looked like an altar, a huge mottled stone head, like a happy Buddhist god with leprosy. It also looked like a lumpy manhole cover, put there to keep whoever's inside from getting out. I tried to breathe beatifically. I thought of Tom, and wanted to ask, "What on earth did Mary do when Jesus was thirteen?"

Here's what I think: She occasionally started gathering rocks.

If we take the incarnation seriously, then even good old Jesus was thirteen once, a human thirteen-year-old. He learned by doing, as we have to. He had to go through adolescence. It must have been awful sometimes. Do you know anyone for whom adolescence was consistently okay? But in his case, we don't know for sure. We see him earlier, in the Bible, at twelve, when he's speaking to the elders in the Temple. He's great with the elders, just as Sam is always fabulous with other grown-ups. They can't believe he's such an easygoing kid, with such good manners. In the Temple, Jesus says things so profound that the elders are amazed. "Who's this kid's teacher?" they wonder. They don't know that Jesus' teacher was the Spirit.

But at the same time he's blowing the elders away, how is Jesus treating his parents? I'll tell you: He's making them crazy. He's ditched them. They can't find him for three days. Some of you know what it's like to not find your kid for three hours. You die. Mary and Joseph have looked everywhere, in the market, at the video arcade. Finally they find him, in the last place they thought to look—the Temple. And immediately, he mouths off: Oh, sorry, sorry, I was busy doing all this other stuff, my father's work. Like, Joseph, you're not my real father— you're not the boss of me. I don't even have to listen to you.

And what is Mary doing this whole time?

Mary's got a rock in her hand.

I turned around. Sam sat grimly, and I fixed him with gimlet eyes, pinning him to the seat until he could see the error of his ways.

It seems idiotic for Sam to challenge me so often, since he has no income to speak of, and he can't drive. I looked at the face in the altar, toothless and muckled, with its folded-over mouth. In the alder branches above me, a little gray bird flitted about, modest but melodious. The leaves of the alder quivered. I started to miss Sam. He's every single good thing, including honest, and openly questioning, and angry, that I love so much. The other day he said, with enormous hostility, "We are the only family I know that doesn't display its china." I responded nicely that we don't have any china, and he said, "That's my point."

The hills behind me were close, curvy and feminine. The quaking leaves of the alder sounded like rain against a skylight.

I looked over at my bad boy. He was staring out the window with resigned misery, as if he were on his way to the dentist. I thought about stoning him. Jesus would have said, "Woe to you, scribes and Pharisees, and tax collectors, and thirteen-year-olds," which means, "You are totally pissing me off." And he'd have said this right before he picked up a rock.

I bet he had a good arm, being a carpenter and all. I bet he could take a kid out at 150 yards. I thought of Sam's most infuriating habits; how snotty he can act, how entitled, his clothes and towels always dropped on the floor; the way he answers the phone, sounding like Henry Kissinger and only pretending to take down messages.

What a mess we are, I thought. But this is usually where any hope of improvement begins, acknowledging the mess. When I am well, I know not to mess with mess right away; I try to let silence and time work their magic. You don't get far through grinding your teeth and heavy breathing. You noodle around, to warm up, and you meander, to find out if there are any improvisations that call to you. In this case, that meant for me to get up and move around.

I decided to get out from under the weight of his gaze and discomfort, and so I lay down beside the log. There were small, antic wildflowers in the grass beside me. I closed my eyes and listened to the little birds, to the alders and the grass. I breathed in the hay smell of the grass, toasty, with the hint of distant forest fires, and lots of sweetness, like clean laundry.

I was still and attentive and I prayed, and eventually some of my anger dissipated. After a while, I heard the car door open. It was as if, once things were more peaceful in me, the deer or the bobcat could come out of the thicket to case the joint. I heard his footsteps approach, and I sat up. When he came over, he was both, deer and bobcat, tentative, dangerous, and teary. He stood a few feet away, looking back at the car.

He sighed and began to speak. "I'm sorry I was such an asshole," he said.

I'd sort of been hoping he'd say something I could report back to my pastor, but I saw how bad he felt, how lonely.

"Okay?" he said.

I shook my head and sighed. "I'm sorry I was such an asshole, too."

He sat down in the dirt, and we talked in a stilted, unhappy way. I practiced being right for a while, and he was sullen; then I practiced being kind. Things improved a bit. My friend Mark, who works with church youth groups, reminded me recently that Sam doesn't need me to correct his feelings. He needs me to listen, to be clear and fair and parental. But most of all he needs me to be alive in a way that makes him feel he will be able to bear adulthood, because he is terrified of death, and that includes growing up to be one of the stressed-out, gray-faced adults he sees rushing around him.

"Now can we go back to Anthony's?" he asked, petulantly. We got up and walked to the car. I draped my arm around his shoulders like a sweater.

eight

sincere
meditations

Sometimes, if you are lucky and brave, you can watch someone who's met with serious illness or loss do the kind of restoration that I suspect we are here on earth to do. If you've ever seen David Roche, the monologist and pastor of the Church of 80% Sincerity, you may have already witnessed this process.

David and I met years ago through a friend we had in common. The first time we spoke was on the phone, and we talked about God for half an hour. David mentioned that he had a facial deformity, and I thought, Well, whatever, and we talked some more. Then he came to my church, and it turned out he had one of the most severe facial deformities I'd ever seen.

He was born with a huge benign tumor on the bottom left side of his face; surgeons tried to remove it when he was very young. In the process, they removed his lower lip, and then gave him such extensive radiation that the lower part of his face stopped growing, and he was covered with plum-colored burns.

David is fifty-five now, with silvery hair and bright blue eyes.

I first saw him perform at a local community center, at a benefit for refugees in Kosovo. He was wearing a plum-purple dress shirt, which exemplifies the tender and jaunty bravery I have come to associate with him. He stepped out onstage before a hundred grown-ups and a dozen children, and stood smiling while people got a good look. Then he suggested we ask him, in a conversational tone and in unison, "David, what happened to your face?" When we did, he explained about the tumor, the surgery, and all those radiation burns.

He told of wanting to form a gang of the coolest disfigured people in the world, like the Phantom of the Opera, the Beast from *Beauty and the Beast,* Freddy

Krueger, and Michael Jackson. They'd go places as a group—bowling, or to a makeover counter at Macy's.

"People assume I had an awful childhood," he continued. "But I didn't. I was loved and esteemed by my parents. My face may be unique, but my experiences aren't. I believe they are universal."

Wouldn't you think that having a face like his totally messed with his adolescent sex life? Of course it did, he said. And he was stocky, too, a chubby little disfigured guy. But these things were not nearly as detrimental as having been raised Catholic, having been, as he put it, an incense survivor.

As he told his stories through a crazy mouth, a jumble of teeth, only one lip, and a too-large tongue, David's voice sounded not garbled but strangely like a burr, that of a Scottish person who'd just had a shot of novocaine.

"We with facial deformities are children of the dark," he said. "Our shadow is on the outside. And we can see in the dark: we can see you, we see you turn away, but one day we finally understand that you turn away not from our faces but from your own fears. From those things inside you that you think mark you as someone unlovable to your family, and society, and even to God.

"All those years, I kept my bad stories in the dark, but not anymore. Now I am stepping out into the light. And this face has turned out to be an elaborately disguised gift from God."

David spoke of the hidden scary scarred parts inside us all, the soul disfigurement, the fear deep within us that we're unacceptable; and while he spoke, his hands moved fluidly in expressions that his face can't make. His hands are beautiful, fair, light as air, light as a ballet dancer's.

He described his first game of spin-the-bottle, when the girl who was chosen to kiss him recoiled in horror, and he said to her, debonairly, "You know you want me." Then he admitted sheepishly that he didn't actually say that for twenty years; but in soul time, it's never too late. He told of loving a teenage girl named Carol, of how it took months to ask her out, and that when he did, she accepted. They went to the movies and afterward sat on his front porch; he kept trying to put his arm around her but couldn't quite do it, so they talked and talked and talked. He wanted to kiss her but was too shy to ask; he was afraid it was like asking her to kiss a monster. Finally she said, "I need to go home now," and he said, "Carol, I want to kiss you," and she said, "David, I thought you'd never ask."

That was a moment of true grace, and from this experience, he built a church inside himself. There is no physical church, but his own life: both his performances and his work teaching people to tell their stories, their marvelous, screwed-up, and often hilarious resurrection stories. Voilà: a church.

"We in the Church of Eighty Percent Sincerity do not believe in miracles," he said. "But we do believe that you have to stay alert, because good things happen. When God opens the door, you've got to put your foot in.

"Eighty percent sincerity is about as good as it's going to get. So is eighty percent compassion. Eighty percent celibacy. So twenty percent of the time, you just get to be yourself."

It's such subversive material, so contrary to everything society leads us to believe—that if you look good, you'll be happy, and have it all together, and you'll be successful and nothing will go wrong and you won't have to die, and the rot won't get in.

In the Church of 80% Sincerity, you definitely don't have to look good, but you *are* supposed to meditate. According to David's instructions, you sit quietly with your eyes closed and you follow your breath in and out of your body, gently watching your mind. Your mantra should go like this: "Why am I doing this? This is such a waste! I have so much to do! My butt itches. . . ." And if you stick to it, he promised, from time to time calm and peace of mind will intrude. After some practice with this basic meditation, you will be able to graduate to panic meditations, and then sex fantasy meditations. And meditations on what to do when you win the lotto.

When David insists you are fine exactly the way you are, you find yourself almost believing him. When he talks about unconditional love, he gives you a new lease on life, because the way he explains it, you may, for the first time, believe that even you could taste of this. As he explains it, in the Church of 80% Sincerity, everyone has come to understand that unconditional love is a reality, but with a shelf life of about eight to ten seconds. Instead of beating yourself up because you feel it only fleetingly, you should savor those moments when it appears. As David puts it, "We might say to our beloved, 'Honey, I've been having these feelings of unconditional love for you for the last eight to ten seconds.' Or 'Darling, I'll love you till the very end of dinner.'"

David has been married to a beautiful woman named Marlena for the last few years. After listening to his lovely words, his magic, this doesn't seem at all strange. There he is, standing in front of a crowd, and everyone can see that just about the worst thing that could happen to a person physically has happened to him. Yet he's enjoying himself immensely, talking about the ten seconds of grace he felt here, the ten seconds he felt there, how those moments filled him and how he makes them last a little longer. Everyone watching gets happy because he's giving instruction on how this could happen for them, too, this militant self-acceptance. He lost the great big outward thing, the good-looking package, and the real parts endured. They shine through like crazy, the brilliant mind and humor, the depth of generosity, the intense blue eyes, those beautiful hands.

The children, sitting in the front rows, get him right away. Maybe they don't have so many overlays yet, of armor and prejudice, so Spirit can reach out and grab them faster. Maybe it's partly that they're sitting so close, but whatever the reason, they gaze up at him as if he were a rock star. "I look different to you now, right?" he asked the kids that first time I saw him, when he was almost finished, and they nodded, especially the teenagers. To be in adolescence is, for most of us, to be facially deformed. David makes you want to help him build a fort under the table with blankets, because it looks like such fun when he does it. He builds the fort, and then lets you lift the blankets and peek in, at him and at you. You laugh with recognition, with relief that your baggage and flaws are not vile, unmentionable. It's like soul aerobics.

"I've been forced to find my inner beauty," he said in closing. "Doing that gave me a deep faith in myself. Eighty percent of the time. And that faith has been a window, so I can see the beauty in you, too. The light in your eyes. Your warmth. So thank you."

There was thunderous applause, and he bowed shyly, ducking his head and then looking up, beaming at us all. He held his palms up as if about to give a benediction. His hands caught the light like those of the youngest child there.

nine

◎

heat

I need to put in a quick disclaimer so that when I say what I'm about to say, you will know that the truest thing in the world is that I love my son more than life itself. I would rather be with him, talk to him, and watch him grow than do anything else on earth. Okay?

So: I woke up one morning not long ago and lay in bed trying to remember whether, the night before, I had actually threatened to have his pets put to sleep, or whether I had only insinuated that I would no longer intercede to keep them alive when, because of his neglect, they began starving to death.

I'm pretty sure I only threatened not to intercede. But there have been other nights when I've made worse threats, thrown toys off the deck into the street, and slammed the door to his room so hard that things fell off his bookshelf. I have screamed at him with such rage for ignoring me that you would have thought he'd tried to set my bed on fire.

He is an unusually good boy at other people's houses. He is the one the other mothers want to have over to play with their children. At other people's homes, my child does not suck the energy and air out of the room. He does not do the same annoying thing over and over and over until his friends' parents ask him through clenched teeth to stop doing it. But at our house—*comment se dit?*—he fucks with me. He can provoke me into a state similar to road rage.

I have felt many times over the years that I was capable of hurting him. I have not done this yet. Or at any rate, I have only hurt him a little—I have spanked him a few times, yanked him, and grabbed him too hard. Through grace and great friends and sobriety, I have managed to stay on this side of the line, sometimes by the skin of my teeth, and, I should add, so far. But while I honestly grieve for injured children, I know all too well how otherwise loving parents have not been able to toe that line.

It's godawful to get so mad at your child. It's miserable whenever it happens, but at least it makes more sense when they are babies and you are awake night after night. When Sam was a colicky baby, it was one thing to discuss my terrible Caliban feelings with friends because I was so exhausted and hormonal and clueless as to how to be a real mother that I believed anyone would understand. No one tells you when you're pregnant how insane you're going to feel after the baby comes, how pathological, how inept and out of control. Or how, when the child is older, you'll still sometimes feel exhausted, hormonal, clueless. You'll still find your child infuriating. And—I will just say it—dull.

A few mothers seem happy with their children all the time, as if they're sailing through motherhood, entranced. But up close and personal, you find that these moms tend to have little unresolved issues: they exercise three hours a day, or they check their husbands' pockets every night, looking for motel receipts. Because moms get very mad; and they also get bored. This is a closely guarded secret; the myth of maternal bliss is evidently so sacrosanct that we can't even admit these feelings to ourselves. But when you mention the feelings to other mothers, they all say, "Yes, yes!" You ask, "Are you ever mean to your children?" "Yes!" "Do you ever yell so meanly that it scares you?" "Yes, yes!" "Do you ever want to throw yourself down the stairs because you're so bored with your child that you can hardly see straight?" "Yes, Lord, yes . . ."

So let's talk about this.

One reason I think we get so angry with our children is that we can. Who else is there that you can talk to like this? Can you imagine saying to your partner, "You get off the phone *now!* No, *not* in five minutes"? Or to a friend, "Get over here, right this second! The longer you make me wait, the worse it's going to be for you." Or to a salesman at Sears who happens to pick up a ringing phone, "Don't you *dare* answer the phone when I'm talking to you."

No, you can't. If regular people spotted your hidden, angry inside self, they'd draw back when they saw you coming. They would see you for what you are—human, flawed, more nuts than had been hoped—and they would probably not want to hire or date you. Of course, most people have such bit parts in your life that they're not around to see the whole erratic panoply that is you. But children, my God—attending to all their needs is so physically and mentally exhausting and unrelenting that our blow-ups may be like working out cramps in our legs.

The tyranny of waking a sleepy child at seven a.m. and hassling him to get clothed and fed in preparation for school means you're chronically tired, resentful, and resented. In this condition, while begging him to put on socks, you are inevitably treated to an endless and intricate précis of *Rugrats*.

This is how Sam started telling me about one ten-minute patch of school day, while I was trying to watch the news: "So Alex says she didn't draw it, and then she goes like she did draw the picture herself, and then he goes like, 'Oh yeah,' and then she goes like, 'Yeah, I asked her to but she said I had to,' and then he goes like, 'Oh, yeah, riiiight,' then I go . . ."

I am not an ageist: If, while I was watching the news, *Jesus* wanted to tell me in great detail how he runs the fifty-yard dash, I'd be annoyed with him, too: "See, most kids start out like this—the first step is a big one, like this—no, watch—and then the second is smaller, like this, and the next—no, watch, my child, I'm almost done—so see, what I do is, I start like everyone else—*watch*—but then my third step is like small, and the next one is bigger, so like, this P.E. teacher who sees me do it goes, 'Whoa, Lord, cool,' and then she goes . . ."

People who don't want children roll their eyes when you complain, because they think you brought this on yourself. The comedienne Rita Rudner once said that she and her husband were trying to decide whether to buy a dog or have a child—whether to ruin their carpets or their lives. People without children tend not to feel very sympathetic. But some of us want children—and what they give is so rich you can hardly bear it.

At the same time, if you need to yell, children are going to give you something to yell about. There's no reasoning with them. If you get into a disagreement with a regular person, you slog through it—you listen to the other person's position, needs, problems—and you arrive at something that is maybe not perfect, but you don't actually feel like hitting the person. But because we are so tired sometimes, when a disagreement starts with our children, we can only flail miserably through time and space and the holes between; and then we blow our top. Say, for instance, that your child is four and going through the stage when he will wear only the T-shirt with the tiger on it. With a colleague, who was hoping you'd come through with the professional equivalent of washing the tiger T-shirt every night, you might be able to explain that you were up until dawn on deadline, or that you have a fever, and so did not get to the laundry. And the colleague might cut you some slack and understand that you simply hadn't had time to wash the tiger shirt, and besides, it's been worn four days in a row now. But your child is apt to—well, let's say, apt not to.

They may be drooling, covered with effluvia, trying to wrestle underpants on over their heads because they think they're shirts, but in the miniature war room of their heads, children know exactly where your nuclear button is. They may ignore you, or seem afflicted by hearing loss, or erupt in fury at you, or weep, but in any case, they're so unreasonable and capable of such meanness that you're stunned and grief-stricken about how much harder it is than you could have imagined. All you're aware of is the big windy gap between you, with your lack of anything left to give, and any solution whatsoever.

Friends without children point out the good news: that kids haven't, thank God, taken all their impulses and learned to disguise them subtly, because it's wonderful for people to be who they really are. And you can say only, "Isn't that the loveliest possible thought you're having?" Because it's not wonderful when kids ignore you, or are being sassy and oppositional. It's not wonderful when you're coping well enough, feeding them, helping them get ready, trying to have them do something in their best interest—telling them, "Zip up the pants, honey, that's not a great look for you"—and then, under the rubric of What Fresh Hell Is This? the afternoon play date calls and cancels, and there's total despair and hysteria because your child is going to have to hang out alone with *you*, horrible you, and he's sobbing as if the dog had died, and you're thinking, "What about all those times this week when the play dates did work out? Do I get any *fucking* credit for that?" And it happens. *Kaboooom*.

It's so ugly and scary for everyone concerned that— well. One of my best friends, the gentlest person I know, once tore the head off his daughter's doll. And then threw it to her, like a baseball. I love that he told me about it when I was despairing about a recent rage at Sam. While I'm not sure what the solution is, I know that what doesn't help is the terrible feeling of isolation, the fear that everyone else is doing better than you.

What has helped me lately was to figure out that when we blow up at our kids, we only think we're going from zero to sixty in one second. Our surface and persona are so calm that when a problem begins, we sound in control when we say, "Now honey, stop that," or "That's enough." But it's only an illusion. In fact, all day we've been nursing anger toward the boss or boyfriend or mother, yet since we can't get mad at nonkid people, we stuff it down. When the problem with your kid starts up, you're really beginning at fifty-nine, but you're not moving. You're at high idle already, yet not aware of how vulnerable and disrespected you already feel. It's your child's bedtime and all you want is for him to go to sleep so you can lie down and stare at the TV—and it starts up. "Mama, I need to talk to you. It's important." So you go in and muster your patience, and you help him with his fears or his thirst, and you go back to the living room and sink into your couch, and then you hear, "Mama? Please come here one more time." You lumber in like you're dragging a big dinosaur tail behind you, and you rub his back for a minute, his sharp angel shoulder blades. The third time he calls, you try to talk him out of needing you, but he seems to have this problem with self-absorption, and he can't hear that you can't be there for him. And you become wordless with rage. You try to breathe, you try everything, and then you blow. You scream, "Fucking dammit! What? *What? What?* Can't you leave me alone for *four* seconds?"

Now your child feels infinitely safer, much more likely to drift off to sleep.

Good therapy helps. Good friends help. Pretending that we are doing better than we are doesn't. Shame doesn't. Being heard does.

The fear is the worst part, the fear about who you secretly think you are, the fear you see in your child's eyes. But underneath the fear I keep finding resilience, forgiveness, even grace. The third time Sam called for me the other night, I finally blew up in the living room, and there was then a great silence in the house, silence like suspended animation: here I'd been praying for silence, and it turns out to be so charged and toxic. I lay on the couch with my hands over my face, shocked by how hard it is to be a parent. And after a minute Sam sidled out, still needing to see me, to snuggle with me, with mean me, needing to find me—like the baby spider pushing in through the furry black legs of the mother tarantula, knowing she's in there somewhere.

ten

hard rain

Everyone has been having a hard time with life this year; not with all of it, just the waking hours. Being awake is the one real fly in the ointment—but it is also when solutions come to us. So many friends died or got sick this year, watched their children go through terrible patches, or lost a lot of money, but on top of it all, like a dental X-ray apron, was the daily depression of life under the Bush White House. "It's hopeless," my boyfriend muttered now and then. One of the savviest political and spiritual people I know said recently, "We will be at war in Iraq for a long time. It's that simple. Resistance is futile." But I decided it was only nearly impossible, and I'll take nearly impossible over futile any day.

Veronica said, in a recent sermon, that you can keep bees in jars without lids, because they'll walk around on the glass floor, imprisoned by the glass surrounding them, when all they'd have to do is look up and they could fly away. So, I thought gamely, we'll look up, we'll get off our asses, or if we are like bees, off our glasses. But this friend who said resistance was futile, who is usually a crabby optimist like me, was terrorized. She was trying to imagine the end of life as we now know it, under a paranoid right-wing government.

She was talking about life in shelters and caves.

Now, this would not work for me. Shelters would be bad enough—a dinner party is already a real stretch—but I don't even remotely have the right personality for cave dwelling. I need privacy and silence most of the time. Also, I hate stalactites. They make me think of Damocles, cave-camping.

Like most people I know, I stepped up my do-good efforts in the weeks before Bush took us to war in Iraq— I spoke out against the war, registered voters, went to demonstrations, sent money to environmental groups, signed petitions, went to visit old people in convalescent homes, flirted with old people on the street, read *The Nation* and Salon, sent more money to the ACLU, Doctors Without Borders, Clowns Without Borders, the Middle East Children's Alliance, the Global AIDS Interfaith Alliance, to anyone who helps kids and poor people. And I planted bulbs, which is a form of prayer.

But the jungle drums grew louder, and nothing seemed to help. What could possibly help during this administration? God only knows. But in any case, we should try to stay on God's good side. It's not hard. God has extremely low standards. Pray, take care of people, be actively grateful for your blessings, give away your money—you're cool. You're in. Nice room in heaven, flossing no longer required—which is what will make it heaven for me. Oh, I mean that, and Jesus.

And then, the rains began again.

I usually welcome the rain, when I'm tired and stressed. Rain suggests that you should go inside, rest, try to stay dry. The scent of rain is fresh and earthy, clean and woolly, of leaves and dirt, wet dogs. We get whiffs of our animal smells, of feet, sweat, and the secret smells of the earth, which she often keeps to herself. Rain gives us back something that has been stolen, a dimension we've been missing—our body, and our soul. Your mind can't give you these. Your sick, worried mind can't heal your sick, worried mind. Well, maybe your mind is lovely and pastoral and you do not suffer from paranoia, hypochondria, a bad attitude, and delusions of victimized grandeur. That is very nice, but we don't want you in our cave after the bombs fall, because you are going to annoy us to death.

It poured.

Hard rain makes a mess, but it also fills in space we usually walk through without even noticing. It makes the stuff we can't usually see—air and wind—visible, and a lot of what we can see catches light. We get wet and cold, and then we get to dry off and be warm again. But with this rain the power started going off and on, and food went bad, and black grosgrain ribbons of ants arrived, and the winds picked up, and suddenly everything was whapping at us.

The storms made life feel like a cyclotron; everyone was mildewing and emotionally ragged, and war was breathing down our necks. At church I heard that the Marin Interfaith Council was sponsoring a peace rally. At this point it was hard to imagine going to the store, let alone into the rain to protest possible war in Iraq. The universe was pulling out all the stops—torrential rains and power outages for days—and it made me crazy, especially when acquaintances would enthuse about how they were enjoying the lack of electricity, how close together it was bringing their families. (Thank you for sharing, but you can't be in our cave, either. You and your families will have to be in solitary, with your little board games.)

It didn't stop raining, and the wind didn't stop blowing, as if there were too many flies and they were beginning to bother the skin of the universe. The universe was flinching and flailing. And you couldn't fix anything. All you could do was help people. You could set up MASH units in your own life, and tend to people through the sacrament of cocoa and videos, and you could send money, and pray. Things were taking their course—I hate that! But you had to let them. I tried to slow down. Then I needed to nap so often that I concluded I had leukemia. Everyone had had such worry and muffled tension for so long, and the exhaustion of held breath, and I felt rashy and overwhelmed, like Harvey Fierstein with poison oak.

The Marin peace march was to be a candlelight vigil. I was frantic to be alone and curled up in bed reading *The New York Times*. I didn't think anyone would show up besides the loyal leaders of Marin's churches and temples and mosques, putting feet to their prayers.

But then I noticed through the windows that it was barely raining and the wind had died down. Some shafts of sun trickled through. Without overthinking things as usual, I got into my car, drove to San Rafael, and pulled into a parking space.

The rain had stopped. I could see a crowd gathering for the march—old and young; middle-aged people with whom my brothers and I had gone to school, who marched against the war in Vietnam and cleaned up oil spills in Bolinas; babies in strollers, dogs in rain gear. It was noisy, and I know a small-town peace march of a thousand people won't change anything, but I swear I could hear God in Her big-mama guise. She said, "Get out of the damn car already." Still, I sat there. I wanted to go back home, and get it together first—get anything together, even dinner for Sam. Was that too much to ask? But here's what Veronica said during the sermon on bees: God doesn't want or expect you to get it together before you come along, because you *can't* get it together until you come along. You can spend half of your time alone, but you also have to be in service, in community, or you get a little funny.

I got out of the car and walked toward the crowd. The grass was wet and my shoes got wet, but I'd forgotten:

You can get wet, it's okay. Our parents said, "Don't go out in the rain, you'll catch your death of cold!"—as if we'd catch dreaded Japanese river fever if our feet got wet. But our parents were wrong. If you march against war when the war is for shitty reasons—oil and reelection and profit—your shoes might get wet, but maybe fewer people will die in Iraq. Somebody handed me a candle. I found an old schoolmate, friends of my parents. I found my pastor, and other people from my church.

It didn't rain again until the march was over. Two thousand of us eventually gathered, and we milled around until night began to fall. Then we lit our candles and marched, talking and singing. When I said I was hungry, someone gave me a hard butterscotch candy. It was so biblical I could hardly bear it. I couldn't see the front of the procession, it was that far away, and I couldn't see the back. It looked like a Bob Dylan concert. The march was quiet, both somber and joyful. Marchers made plans to meet in San Francisco on a day of mass national demonstrations. This was the happiest I'd felt in a long time. Later that night it rained again, soft, slow, silvery rain, but I was at home by then, warm and dry. In the morning when the sun came up, the light of the new day was faint and clear.

eleven

◉

good friday
world

There is the most ancient of sorrows in the world again, dead civilians and young soldiers. None of us knows quite what to make of things, or what to do. Since the war started last week, the days feel like midnight on the Serengeti, dangers everywhere, some you can see, but most hidden. The praying people I know pray for the lives of innocent people and young Americans to be spared, for peace and sanity to be restored on the global field. Everything feels crazy. But on small patches of earth all over, I can see just as much messy mercy and grace as ever: yesterday at Sam's school, for instance, the kinder-garteners and first-graders were outside when a dozen military planes flew overhead. The children knew we were at war, and were afraid, but when their teacher, Miss Peggy, told them that they were safe, that the planes were going to the Middle East, far away, the children relaxed. They watched more planes fly over. Then one smart child began to worry that there might be children in the Middle East, too, but that maybe these pilots didn't know that. The children started to fret. Miss Peggy could not lie and say there were no children in the places where the planes were going. So she and the children got a giant sheet of paper, and the kids drew a huge peace dove on it, flying over children. They got some older kids to help, including Sam, and they all signed their names. The kids kept telling Miss Peggy that the pilots must not have known—otherwise they would never go to a country where they might accidentally bomb children.

What are you supposed to do, when what is happening can't be, and the old rules no longer apply? I remember this feeling when my mother was in the last stages of Alzheimer's, when my brothers and I needed so much more information to go on than we had—explanations, plans, a tour guide, and hope that it really wasn't going to be that bad. But then it *was* that bad, and then some, and all we could do was talk, and stick together. We managed

to laugh at ourselves and at her, and at the utter hopelessness of it all, and we sought wise counsel—medical, financial, spiritual. I prayed for her to die in her sleep, I prayed
that I'd never have to take the cat out of her arms and put
her in a home. A nurse summoned from the Alzheimer's
Association entered into the mess with us. We said, "We
don't know what we're doing. We don't know if we
should put her in a home, and if so, when. We don't know
what's true anymore." The nurse asked gently, "How
could you know?"

That one sentence, more than any other, saw me
through, every step of the way. We kept hobbling forward, able to do only the next right thing. I remembered
a decal I had once seen, of a gorilla, with the caption:
"The law of the American jungle: Remain calm, share
your bananas." That's what we did—tried to make one
another laugh and stay calm, and shared our bananas.
And when the time came to know what to do, we did. I
took the cat out of my mother's arms; we put her in a
home. It was a nightmare. It killed something in us, yet we
came through.

A friend called today and said that since the war has
begun, she finds herself inside a black hole half the time.
"What if we gave fifty percent of our discretionary budget

to the world's poor," she said, "and then counted on the moral power of that action to protect us?" Good Lord: What can you say in the face of such innocence?

"You didn't stop taking those meds, did you?" I asked.

This made her laugh. "I just don't feel like I can get through the day. Even though I know I will."

Like her, I am depressed and furious. I often feel like someone from the Book of Lamentations. The best thing I've heard lately is the Christian writer Barbara Johnson's saying that we're Easter people, living in a Good Friday world.

I don't have the right personality for Good Friday, for the crucifixion: I'd like to skip ahead to the resurrection. In fact, I'd like to skip ahead to the resurrection vision of one of the kids in our Sunday school, who drew a picture of the Easter Bunny outside the tomb: everlasting life, and a basket full of chocolates. *Now* you're talking.

In Jesus' real life, the resurrection came two days later, but in our real lives, it can be weeks, years, and you never know for sure that it will come. I don't have the right personality for the human condition, either. But I believe in the resurrection, in Jesus', and in ours. The trees, so stark and gray last month, suddenly went up as if in flame, but instead in blossoms and leaves—poof! Like someone opening an umbrella. It's often hard to find similar dramatic evidence of rebirth and hope in our daily lives.

What is there to do in such difficult, violent times? I try to follow my own advice to take short assignments, and do shitty first drafts of my work, and most of all, to take things day by day. Today I am going to pray that our soldiers come home soon. I am going to pray for the children of American and Iraqi soldiers, for the innocent Iraqi people, for the POWs, for humanitarian aid, and for our leaders. I am going to pray for the children and youth in Oakland and East Palo Alto and Palestine and Israel. I am going to pray to forgive one person today—to give up a soupçon of hostility. Or maybe for the willingness to really forgive someone today—Bush, for instance, who got us into this mess—even though I do not expect it to go well. Forgiveness is not my strong suit.

You can always begin by lighting a candle. Since the United States went to war in Iraq, I've been thinking about A. J. Muste, who during the Vietnam War stood in front of the White House night after night with a candle. One rainy night, a reporter asked him, "Mr. Muste, do you really think you are going to change the policies of this country by standing out here alone at night with a candle?"

"Oh," Muste replied, "I don't do it to change the country, I do it so the country won't change me."

I am going to send checks to people and organizations I trust, including Oakland's progressive representative Barbara Lee, who speaks for me. I will ask her to send the check on to someone who is nurturing children in the inner city, because this nation's black and Hispanic kids will be the hardest hit by wartime deficit spending. I am going to buy myself a pair of beautiful socks, and my son some new felt-tip pens.

I am going to walk to the library, because my church is too far away to go to on foot. And it's so beautiful out. The hills of my town are lush and green and dotted with wildflowers. The poppies have bloomed, and as summer approaches, five o'clock is no longer the end of the world. I am going to check out a collection of *Goon Show* scripts, and a volume of Mary Oliver poems. Libraries make me think kindly of my mother. I am not sure if this will lead me directly to the soupçon of forgiveness, but you never know. You take the action, and the insight follows. It was my mother who taught me how to wander through the racks of the Belvedere–Tiburon library, and wander through a book, letting it take me where it would. She and my father took me to the library every week when I was little. One of her best friends was the librarian. They both taught me that if you insist on having a destination when you come into a library, you're shortchanging yourself. They read to live, the way they also went to the beach, or ate delicious food. Reading was like breathing fresh ocean air, or eating tomatoes from old man Grbac's garden. My parents, and librarians along the way, taught me about the space between words; about the margins, where so many juicy moments of life and spirit and friendship could be found. In a library, you can find small miracles and truth, and you might find something that will make you laugh so hard that you will get shushed, in the friendliest way. I have found sanctuary in libraries my whole life, and there is sanctuary there now, from the war, from the storms of our families and our own minds. Libraries are like mountains or meadows or creeks: sacred space. So this afternoon, I'll walk to the library.

I am going to pray for our president to believe that all people deserve to be fed, and to try to make that a reality. Bush believes in serving the poor, but only when they are the "deserving" poor. What on earth does that mean? If I were more spiritually evolved, I would mail him a friendly card, because if you want to change the way you feel about people, you have to change the way you treat them.

143

I know that Bush is family, and that I am supposed to love him, but I hate this—he is a dangerous member of the family, like a Klansman, or Osama bin Laden. Maybe I can't exactly forgive him right now, in the sense of canceling my resentment and judgment. But maybe I can simply acknowledge what is true, spiritually—that he gets to come to the table and eat, too; that I would not let him starve. In heaven, I may have to sit next to him, and in heaven, I know, I will love him. On earth, however, when I consider that he is my brother, and I am to love him, I'm reminded of the old Woody Allen line that someday the lion shall lie down with the lamb, but the lamb is not going to get any sleep. So I will pray to stop hating him, and that he will not kill so many people, today.

I am going to try to pay attention to the spring, and look up at the hectic trees. Amid the smashing and crashing and terrible silences, the trees are in blossom, and it's soft and warm and bright. I am going to close my eyes and listen. During the children's sermon last Sunday, the pastor asked the kids to close their eyes for a moment—to give themselves a time-out—and then asked them what they had heard. They heard birds, and radios, dogs barking, cars, and one boy said, "I hear the water at the edge of things." I am going to listen for the water at the edge of things today.

I keep remembering the inhabitants of those islands in the South Pacific where the United States air force set up a base of operations during World War II. The islanders loved the air force's presence, all that loud, blinding illumination from above, a path of klieg lights descending on their land. They believed it was divine, because there was no other way to understand all that energy, and after the air force left, they created a fake runway with candles and torches and pyres, and awaited its return. I am going to pray for the opposite of loud crashing lights, however. I am going to notice the lights of the earth, the sun and the moon and the stars, the lights of our candles as we march, the lights with which spring teases us, the light that is already present. If the present is really all we have, then the present lasts forever. And that, today, will be the benediction.

twelve

◉

diamond heart

If I could write only one more story in my whole life, it would be this:

Sam's wrestling practice was canceled one recent afternoon, and he was driving me crazy with his pent-up energy. I was puttering around the house, which is my main spiritual practice, and he kept ambushing me with demands for food or attention, and demonstrations of wrestling menace—grabbing at me as if to put me in a hammer hold, or coming at me as if to pile-drive me into the kitchen floor like Hulk Hogan: "I'm not going to hurt you," he reassured me, like a serial killer, flinging his leg around the backs of my knees so that I was afraid they would buckle. I'm fifty, but already I'm turning into an old dog, with poor vision, dysplasia, achy knees, a weak back, and flatulence, while he's raw robust animal health. Something in him wants to flip me, Samoan-drop me into the carpet. I put up puny Rose Kennedy dukes and asked him if he wanted to go for a hike on the mountain. He said yes.

He's two inches taller than I am. The other day he gave me a good-night hug and noticed that he was looking down into my eyes.

"Wow," he said, stepping back. "When did this happen? You're like a little gnome to me now."

I am shrinking and he is shooting up, but we share that on the inside we both feel no different from children and we both get a lot of exercise. I am positive of only a few things in life, and one is that if you want to have a decent middle and old age, you have to get exercise almost every day. All the older people who are thriving have stayed physically active—there are exceptions, and everyone knows someone who smoked two packs a day and had a few social beers with breakfast every morning who lived to be eighty-five, but you have to assume that this won't be you. You have to assume that without exercise, you'll be the dead one, or if you're lucky, the one in diapers, with a cannula up your nose.

We headed out to Deer Park, which is the northern face of Mount Tamalpais, about half a mile from our house. I hiked on the southern side of the mountain with my father my whole life until he died. As young children, my brothers and I straggled along behind him, but when I got older, he and I would stride up steep hills together, sometimes in silence, other times talking, about books, politics, culture, family. I'd mention books or poems that I knew would please him—Kazantzakis, "Prufrock"—and sometimes before a hike I would read criticism or introductions to works so I could keep up in conversation. I lived for his admiration. I didn't want to instill this need to impress in Sam, and luckily, "impress" might be a bit strong to describe how Sam acts around me. He loves me, most of the time, and thinks I'm hilarious, but he doesn't perform the way I did: he doesn't study for our conversations, he doesn't chat up my friends, he doesn't read books so that we can discuss them. In fact, he reads very few books. He reads what he wants, namely magazines in areas I have no opinions or particular interest in: motherboards for his computer, bike frames. I'd always imagined Sam and me strolling along together, talking like my dad and I used to talk, about intellectual things. But I get something better. I get this:

"Darling, did you finish *Romeo and Juliet*?" I asked this at the trailhead, hoping to kick off a bookish discussion. "And did you like it?"

"Yep. I loved it."

"Tell me what you loved."

"Great writing. Clever story." That was it.

We set out on the fire road that leads to a steep trail, with Lily racing ahead.

"Did you ever notice how much Lily looks like Benicio Del Toro?" Sam asked. It's true.

He and Lily dropped behind me, and I walked along lost in my thoughts and the beauty of the woods. After a while, I reached the high trail that meanders through bay and laurel groves. You get various climates here on the mountain: first, in the English dappled shade, it's cool and it smells like spring and mulch; a few minutes later, you come out from under the trees and you're in Sicily, in bright blue heat.

Hearing a commotion, I turned to find Sam. He was bashing the ground with a branch, whacking at the low-hanging branches as if they were piñatas. Rather than give a short talk on honoring the ecosystem that he and his classmates have studied extensively, I continued walking. I rest in silence and music and long strides, while Sam rests in noise and motion.

After a moment he stopped his whacking, and the silence was broken only by birdsong, our footsteps, and invisible animals moving around in the fallen leaves and twigs. Then Sam started whistling. His grandfather taught him to whistle when he was four—his adopted grandfather, Rex, my father's best friend of thirty years. My father died ten years before Sam was born, and I was still struggling with an achy emptiness, a feeling that my life had been diminished by half at his death. How would my books and Sam even matter if my father wasn't around to be proud? Now he's been dead for as long as I knew him alive, and sometimes when I've done something fabulous, I feel like a gymnast who has performed a flawless routine in an empty auditorium.

Sam looks a lot like my father did as a boy. Sam also looks like his own father. The first time Sam and I took a walk with Sam's father, John led the way through the woods behind his father's house. Sam walked shyly, ten feet or more behind his dad, and I took up the rear, feeling terror and grief that I was having to share my son. But it cheered me to hear him whistling away. It wasn't that he didn't feel shy and nervous; it was just that Rex had taught him how to whistle.

Rex was one of three men who helped raise Sam during his first five years, the others being my brother Stevo, who taught Sam how to wrassle and goof off, and his unofficial big brother, Brian, who was bathing and diapering him when he was two weeks old, and taking him on adventures ever since—canoeing, train rides, farmers' markets. Rex's specialties were camping and workshop. They spent hours in Rex's workroom when Sam was young, hammering, nailing, talking, silent. Rex discovered that Sam connects with his own spirit most when he is working with his hands. He would study a nail, or a washer, as if he were holding a butterfly.

Sam dropped back from me on the trail, then caught up, an edgy psycho-scamper. He stabbed the air with his sword, so joyous, so masculine. He's always picked up anything that can be used to smash other things, or to make bombs, or to destroy piles of leaves or sand or stones. He's a closed current of energy, like those flashlights you squeeze to make the wires connect inside, and then they pour forth their light. He walked with me for a few minutes in silence. He's transparent at these times, like a baby, without any of the barriers or labyrinths people set up later, out of fear.

Before Sam was born, people told me how utterly transparent with beauty babies could be. I have a photograph on the wall in my study of a baby in Sudan, breast-feeding, and she looks like chocolate, wrapped in a blue and lavender napkin, pressed into what little we can see of her mother's brown-black breast. This is a universal baby, a safe baby. I had thought Sam would be more like this, more of the time. I saw the same flatness in his nose when he nursed, like the Sudanese baby trying to get as close as possible to what nourished her, and the same deliciousness of baby arms. But the clutch of her fingers should have tipped me off—that grasping and clutching might come with the territory, grasping and clutching at you, and then pushing you away—and the openness of the baby's ear—babies are listening, can hear, and will one day use what they hear against you.

Smash, bash, whack. Sam swung at branches above him as if delivering forehand volleys. Sometimes I worry that he takes such joy in wrecking things. When he was two, being awful and destructive on every level of his pitiful, loathsome, poopy existence, I told my friend Pammy, calmly, "He's a bad person. He's already ruined."

Pammy said something that I have clung to like the last heel of bread: "Sam has a deep core of sweetness within him." She was right. He's deeply compassionate, and fair, but he also loves knives, and air-soft guns, and paintball guns, and Ninja blades, and violence. Maybe it was inconsistent for us to watch *Touched by an Angel* together, right before we watched *South Park*. Maybe it confused him that we went to church on Sundays and then watched *The Sopranos*.

He has always said the funniest things. Until he was five, he couldn't say *l*'s properly. He pronounced them *y*. Yeaf, yunch, yove, the Yord, and Sam Yamott. One day he came home from school and said slowly that he had lllloved his lllunch. His teacher had finally taught him *l*'s. He ran to the house next door to show off for the teenagers he adored. It was a bittersweet moment: Your kid can't get a job on CNN if he can't say his *l*'s, but now he's growing up; he'll be dating soon, and mouthing off and sneering when he's furious. And that has come true, though now he's the teenager all the little kids love.

He still says things that I scribble down on index cards. Just this morning as I drove him to school, we were talking about politics, and he said, "Mom, you know— you have a very rich vocabulary." He can make words all his own. "Random" is the latest favorite. I'll say something I've been meaning to tell him all day, and he'll look at me askance and say, "Wow, that's a little random." Driving along with him and his friend Nick the other day, I told Nick, "You know, I'll always be one of the adults who is on your side, if you need me." He replied, "Oh, thanks, Annie," and there was silence in the car until Sam said, "God, *that* was random."

Now Sam pushed the tip of his branch into the pebbly ground like a divining rod, splitting the road in two, making a great noise unto the Yord. He exerts tremendous energy, and it builds up and he sends it forth with his tools, his swords. It's art, it's an installation, it's the American way: "We're big and strong and male, and this thing is about to get seriously small, and be in shreds, because I am about to heavily fuck with it." He finds where something has a weak spot, picks up a branch, and jabs it, like a physical yell.

He can say terrible, mean things to me, and then, a few hours later, be so kind and contrite that it brings tears to my eyes. He was always this way, accepting and fair, capable of casual meanness and extraordinary empathy. When he was seven and we started looking for his father, I asked him what he would do if it turned out that his father was strange, or standoffish, and Sam said genuinely, "Oh, *I* wouldn't care. I wouldn't care if he was a crook. I wouldn't care if he had a gun. *I* wouldn't care if he cut down trees and didn't re*plant*." You can see that we live in an ecologically correct area.

I pulled over by the side of the road to write this down, pretending I was making a shopping list. I always write down his exact words. He is an exact person, as we all are, even though I sense that there is only one of us, that we are mosaic chips of that One. Sam is very stylish, oddly enough, as I'm not stylish at all. His hair always looks good. And I was always a great student, whereas he isn't, in the classic sense, of a student who studies hard, likes to read, and hands in homework. He's a great student in the reform sense: he's fascinated by life, he's funny, and he participates eagerly in discussions. I've never yelled at anyone in my whole life except for him, and he yells at me, too. We fight about homework and his mouthiness and the laundry. I no longer wash his dirty clothes for him, because he will not put them away, so he does his own, and keeps the clean clothes unfolded in a basket, with an empty basket beside it so he can transfer clothes rapidly from one basket to another while looking for something to wear—like a fabric Slinky. There's a third basket, for dirty clothes, which is usually empty, as the dirty clothes are strewn all over his bedroom floor.

Sam began chucking rocks into the creek, and Lily barked at them loyally, as if shaking her fist—"and *stay* away!" I listened to the splashes of the rocks he was pitching, aiming at other rocks, or at unseen enemies, creation and destruction in the same breath. I heard the knock of one stone hitting another, and fingered the diamond heart that I wear on a thin gold chain around my neck. He bought the heart for me last December, at the Mervyn's holiday sale. A few days before Christmas, he thrust the box at me. I turned away from it, because I wanted to wait till Christmas, but he ripped the wrapping paper off, then opened the box for me. There was a small gold heart studded with diamonds, the exact piece of jewelry I had always wanted. He watched me with enormous pride and pleasure. "One hundred fifty-nine dollars at Mervyn's, Mom," he said, proudly, and added, "Retail."

I asked a friend of mine who practices a spiritual path called Diamond Heart to explain the name, because I instinctively know that both Sam and I have, or are, diamond hearts. My friend said our hearts are like diamonds because they have the capacity to express divine light, which is love; we not only are portals for this love, but are made of it. She said we are made of light, our hearts faceted and shining, and I believe this, to a point: I disagree with her saying we are beings of light wrapped in bodies that merely seem dense and ponderous, yet actually are made of atoms and molecules, with infinite space and light between them. It must be easy for her to believe this, as she is thin, and does not have children. But I can meet her halfway: I think we are diamond hearts, wrapped in meatballs.

I would call my path Diamond Meatball: people would comfort and uplift one another by saying, "There's a diamond in there *some*where."

Still, on better days, I see us as light in containers, like those pierced tin lanterns that always rust, that let the candlelight shine out in beautiful snowflake patterns.

Sam raced ahead of me, and then slowed down, looking back to gloat at the distance he'd put between us. He's very competitive, like me. Then he waved nicely, and went on. Oh, Sam: I worry that I was either too strict, or not strict enough. I'm not quite sure which. I've given him a lot of freedom—he can take public transportation all over the county—but I'm strict about manners, and church. You have to contain children, or you ruin them, and no one will ever want you to come visit. But children go ballistic when their unfettered spirits feel constricted and picked on by horrible you. They like you less, but if you don't do it, they feel wounded. "You shouldn't have even had children," they'll say with contempt. They'll comment on your clothes or your butt, in public, or your hair or your grooming.

Once when Sam was twelve or so, we were standing in line at the movies and I found him staring at me judgmentally.

"What?" I asked.

"When you got your dreadlocks, you made a commitment to keep them *groomed*," he said. "But you've let them get all fuzzy."

It's a mixed grill of sweet and nourishing and intolerable, like life. You and your bright, bonny child walk hand in hand to the park, and then, while sitting on a bench, you see his delight in hurting another kid. Kids go right for the vulnerability in other kids, ganging up on the weakest, ditching, or snatching things away. Life is not what one had in mind; it's not the TV sitcoms or the commercials, or the photo of the Sudanese baby. It's punishing. It makes you want to punish back.

There are times when Sam is so mouthy that all I can do is pray for a sense of humor and absurdity, even if it's the size of a mustard seed. Otherwise, I look at C-minuses on progress reports, and see him at thirty taking orders at Taco Bell. If he could even get that job, with his handwriting. Or he is sent home from school for participating in a mudfight, and I think, Timothy McVeigh. Or I realize: I don't like this child, I shouldn't have had a kid, it's all hopeless. All I can do is pray: *Help!*

Sam, Lily, and I walked together in the shade of the trees for a while. I looked over a few times and smiled at him. Left to my own devices, I find myself hurrying along with my head down, shoulders hunched, my hands grasped behind my back like Groucho Marx. But Sam beside me and the songs of unseen birds make me look up and around, make me notice the patches of blue sky between the dense branches. Maybe this is what grace is, the unseen sounds that make you look up. I think it's why we are here, to see as many chips of blue sky as we can bear. To find the diamond hearts within one another's meatballs. To notice flickers of the divine, like dust motes on sunbeams in your dusty kitchen. Without all the shade and shadows, you'd miss the beauty of the veil. The shadow is always there, and if you don't remember it, when it falls on you and your life again, you're plunged into darkness. Shadows make the light show. Without shadows, we'd see only what a friend of mine refers to as "all that goddamn light."

Sam ran ahead again, picking up rocks as he went. Lily chased after him. He creates a force field around him that nothing can breach, that comes out of the very center of him. Everything is concentrated on that torque. I watched him go. I've been watching him go since he learned how to crawl. Sometimes I didn't watch closely enough, and he got hurt—he burned his hand badly once, and he split his eyebrow open on a coffee table, and he and his friends got drunk a few times last summer. I'm always afraid he'll end up as I did, stoned and drunk for many years, sick in the mornings. "Don't worry, Mom," he says, but that's what I used to tell my parents. I tell him what Chef in *South Park* said. "Children . . . There's a time and place for doing drugs, and it's called college." He smiles, and like a hawk I watch him go, and watch him go, watch him go.

Heartbreaking things have befallen some of the children we know, even when their parents kept their eyes open: cystic fibrosis, truancy, homelessness, alcohol, drugs. Most of them have come through, though, scarred and shaking their heads. Sometimes things were so awful for friends of mine that I thought it was all over. Rocks came tumbling down on them, on their lives, yet with help, they endured. In some cases, the rocks continue to fall, but even so, when it looks to the outside world as if they are doomed, it turns out that something inside is slowly being fused back together. They find an underground, wiggly strength.

Sam stomped ahead of me like a mountain goat to the top of the hill, and waited. When I caught up with him, he stuck his branch out—to pull me up, I thought—but he pantomimed a swordfight and poked me.

"God," I said involuntarily, knowing it was an accident. "Can you cut me a little slack?"

"I'm sorry. My bad." He always says that, like a baby Rastafarian: "My bad." He reached out and pulled me the last few steps to the top. I walked until I came upon the view of a million fleecy trees, the foothills of Mount Tam. I sat down.

"What if there's another 9/11?" he said.

"What made you think about *that*?" I asked.

He shrugged. "Is there any situation where you would kill Lily?"

"Of course not, unless she was very ill."

"What if there was another 9/11?" he asked. "And we didn't have any food. You wouldn't kill *Lily* to feed me?"

"Sam." I laughed, but he was serious. "Okay, honey," I said. "I'll kill Lily."

"If there was nothing left, would you let me kill you and eat you?"

"Sure, honey."

"I wouldn't want you to die, necessarily. I might just cut off your arm to survive."

"Well. Help yourself."

"What if there is another attack, here?"

"Then we'll all band together and share what we have."

"Will we have to share with Uncle and Jamie?" He gave me his trademark look, a long, slow sideways glance. He was suppressing a smile.

"Of course—he's my brother!"

"Yeah, but Stevo and Jamie eat so much. And now with the baby? Too many mouths to feed!" Sam can always make me laugh. I know where he got his gallows humor. I can see myself so clearly in him, many of my worst traits, some of my goodness. I also can still see many of Sam's ages in him. New parents grieve as their babies get bigger, because they cannot imagine the child will ever be so heartbreakingly cute and needy again. Sam is a swirl of every age he's ever been, and all the new ones, like cotton candy, like the Milky Way. I can see the stoned wonder of the toddler, the watchfulness of the young child sopping stuff up, the busy purpose and workmanship of the nine-year-old. I see him and his oldest friend, Jack, outside working on an electric fence, taping six-volt batteries to it, using endless amounts of duct tape and wires and switches. I see him fashioning robots at the kitchen table with bits of junk, a glue gun, and a nine-volt battery. I see him at my desk, making a small electric fan that works. He can get most of his inventions to light up, or walk: he invents the same way I write—as Virginia Woolf said, "Arrange whatever pieces come your way." Sam creates things out of whatever grabs his attention—bits of plastic, toys, cloth, balloons, fool's gold, mirrors, batteries.

He came and stood beside me, silent. "What do you think about when you come here?"

"This is where I most feel the presence of God. Except for church."

He looked out at the mountainside, at a hawk, at turkey vultures circling, at birds singing in the brush. "Can I sit in your yap?" he asked.

I was sitting cross-legged in the dirt, and he plopped down into my lap. He weighed a ton. I couldn't have gotten up if I'd wanted to. I held him loosely and smelled his neck. Sometimes when I dream about him, he's in danger, he's doing things that are too risky, but most of the time he's stomping around or we're just hanging out together. Sometimes I dream about him when he was younger, and I remember it with such sweetness that it wakes me.

thirteen

untitled

I was at a wedding the other day with a lot of women in their twenties and thirties. Many wore sexy dresses, their youthful skin aglow. And even though I was twenty to thirty years older than they, a little worse for wear, a little tired, and overwhelmed by the loud music, I was smiling.

I smiled with a secret smile of pleasure in being older, fifty plus change, which can no longer be considered extremely late youth, or even early middle age. But I would not give back a year of life I've lived.

Age has given me what I was looking for my entire life—it has given me *me*. It has provided time and experience and failures and triumphs and time-tested friends who have helped me step into the shape that was waiting for me. I fit into me now. I have an organic life, finally, not necessarily the one people imagined for me, or tried to get me to have. I have the life I longed for. I have become the woman I hardly dared imagine I could be. There are parts I don't love—until a few years ago, I had no idea that you could have cellulite on your stomach—but not only do I get along with me most of the time now, I am militantly and maternally on my own side.

Left to my own devices, would I trade this for firm thighs, fewer wrinkles, a better memory?

You bet I would. That is why it's such a blessing that I'm not left to my own devices. I have amazing friends. I have a cool kid, a sweet boyfriend, darling pets. I've learned to pay attention to life, and to listen. I'd give up all this for a flatter belly? Only about a third of the time.

I still have terrible moments when I despair about my body—time and gravity have not made various parts of it higher and firmer. But those are just moments now—I used to have *years* when I believed I was more beautiful if I jiggled less, if all parts of my body stopped moving when I did. But I know two things now that I didn't at thirty:

That when we get to heaven, we will discover that the appearance of our butts and our skin was 127th on the list of what mattered on this earth. And that I am not going to live forever. Knowing these things has set me free.

I am thrilled—ish—for every gray hair and sore muscle, because of all the friends who didn't make it, who died too young of AIDS and breast cancer. I'm decades past my salad days, and even past the main course: maybe I'm in my cheese days—sitting atop the lettuce leaves on the table for a while now with all the other cheese balls, but with much nutrition to offer, and still delicious. Or maybe I'm in my dessert days, the most delicious course. Whatever you call it, much of the stuff I used to worry about has subsided—what other people think of me, and of how I am living my life. I give these things the big shrug. Mostly. Or at least eventually. It's a huge relief.

I became more successful in my forties, but that pales in comparison with the other gifts of my current decade—how kind to myself I have become, what a wonderful, tender wife I am to myself, what a loving companion. I prepare myself tubs of hot salt water at the end of the day, and soak my tired feet. I run interference for myself when I am working, like the wife of a great artist would—"No,

I'm sorry, she can't come. She's working hard these days, and needs a lot of down time." I live by the truth that "No" is a complete sentence. I rest as a spiritual act.

I have grown old enough to develop radical acceptance. I insist on the right to swim in warm water at every opportunity, no matter how I look, no matter how young and gorgeous the other people on the beach are. I don't think that if I live to be eighty, I'm going to wish I'd spent more hours in the gym or kept my house a lot cleaner. I'm going to wish I had swum more unashamedly, made more mistakes, spaced out more, rested. On the day I die, I want to have had dessert. So this informs how I live now.

I have survived so much loss, as all of us have by our forties—my parents, dear friends, my pets. Rubble is the ground on which our deepest friendships are built. If you haven't already, you will lose someone you can't live without, and your heart will be badly broken, and you never completely get over the loss of a deeply beloved person. But this is also good news. The person lives forever, in your broken heart that doesn't seal back up. And you come through, and you learn to dance with the banged-up heart. You dance to the absurdities of life; you dance to the minuet of old friendships.

I danced alone for a couple of years, and came to believe that I might not ever have a passionate romantic relationship—might end up alone! I'd always been terrified of this. But I'd rather not ever be in a couple, or ever get laid again, than be in a toxic relationship. I spent a few years celibate. It was lovely, and it was sometimes lonely. I had surrendered; I'd run out of bullets. I learned to be the person I wished I'd meet, at which point I found a kind, artistic, handsome man. When we get out of bed, we hold our lower backs, like Walter Brennan, and we laugh, and bring each other the Advil.

Younger women worry that their memories will begin to go. And you know what? They will. Menopause has not increased my focus and retention as much as I'd been hoping. But a lot is better-off missed. A lot is better not gotten around to.

I know many of the women who were at the wedding fear getting older, and I wish I could gather them together, and give them my word of honor that every one of my friends loves being older, loves being in her forties, fifties, sixties, seventies. My aunt Gertrud is eighty-five and leaves us behind in the dust when we hike. Look, my feet hurt some mornings, and my body is less forgiving when I exercise more than I am used to. But I love my life more, and me more. I'm so much juicier. And as that old saying goes, it's not that I think less of myself, but that I think of myself less often. And that feels like heaven to me.

fourteen

'joice to the world

My pastor Veronica said yesterday that God constantly tells us to rejoice, but to do that, to get our 'joice *back,* we need to have had joy before. And it's never been needed as badly as now, when the world is hurting so badly, because joy is medicine.

San Quentin may not seem the obvious place to go searching for joy, but my friend Neshama and I went there last week to teach inmates how to tell stories. I would work with them on the craft of writing, while Neshama, who found her voice through the oral tradition, would pass along what she's learned in her work at a guild where people teach one another to tell crafted stories from the stage.

I was glad to be there, for a number of reasons. First of all, because Jesus said that whatever you did to the least of his people, you did to him, and the lifers in penitentiaries are the leastest people in this country. Just look to see whose budgets are being cut these days—the old, the crazies, the children in Head Start—and that's where Jesus will be. He also promised that God forgives the unlovable and the unforgivable, which means most of us—the lifers, me, maybe you.

Second, my father had taught English and writing at San Quentin during the 1950s and 1960s. He published stories in *The New Yorker* about his students, and then wrote a biography of San Quentin; I grew up hearing and reading about his students and the place itself. He did not bog down in complex moral and ethical matters—victims' rights, recidivism. He just taught the prisoners to read good books, to speak English, and to write. My father treated them with respect and kindness, his main philosophical and spiritual position being, Don't be an asshole. My brothers and I stood outside the gates of San Quentin with him and his friends over the years, in protest and silent witness whenever someone was going to be gassed.

And last, I was happy to be there because one of the inmates, Wolf, the head of the Vietnam vets group there, had asked me to help some of his friends with their writing.

I had been inside the grounds for worship services at night, but had never visited during the day. When we went, it was pouring rain. Waiting outside the walls with Neshama, two San Quentin English teachers, and a friend from church, I felt aware of the violence and fear of the world. I hardly know what to feel most days, except grief and bug-eyed paranoia. But my faith tells me that God has skills, ploys, and grace adequate to bring light into the present darkness, into families, prisons, governments.

San Quentin is on a beautiful piece of land in Marin County, on the east shore of San Francisco Bay, with lots of sun, views of the bridges, hills, windsurfers. I tried not to worry as we waited. On Sundays, Veronica kept repeating what Paul and Jesus always said: Don't worry! Don't be so anxious. In dark times, give off light. Care for the least of God's people. She quoted the Reverend James Forbes as saying, "Nobody gets into heaven without a letter of reference from the poor." Obviously, "the poor" includes prisoners.

Jesus had an affinity for prisoners. He had been one, after all. He must have often felt anxiety and isolation in jail, but he always identified with the prisoners. He made a point of befriending the worst and most hated, because his message was that no one was beyond the reach of divine love, despite society's way of stating the opposite. God: what a nut.

Finally, we stood outside an inner gate, showed our IDs to the guards, and got our hands stamped with fluorescent ink. "You don't glow, you don't go," said one cheerful, pockmarked guard, which was the best spiritual advice I'd had in a long time.

As we stepped into a holding pen, my mind spun with worries about being taken hostage, having a shotgun strapped to my head with duct tape. I don't think Jesus would have been thinking these same thoughts: everything in him reached out with love and mercy and redemption. He taught that God is able to bring life from even the most death-dealing of circumstances, no matter where the terror alert level stands.

Our group was allowed to view the outer walls of the prison, which was built in 1852. San Quentin possesses great European beauty—ancient-looking walls, elegant gun towers. It's like a set from Edgar Allan Poe. Someone with the right attitude could do something really nice with this place, something more festive. It could be a cute bed-and-breakfast, say. Or a brewery. I did not know who would be inside, only that most of the convicts were murderers serving life sentences. I imagined that some would be sullen and shifty-eyed, and others charming cons, trying to win me over so I would marry them and get them better lawyers, and consort with them on alternate Tuesdays. I knew there'd be camaraderie, violence, and redemption inside, because I'd read my father's account and the accounts of others. But those were written years ago, when you could still believe in caring for prisoners without being accused of being soft on crime.

Jesus was soft on crime. He'd never have been elected anything.

In the courtyard, we were met by several staff people, and then by Wolf and two of his friends, all polite and clean-shaven, with Vietnam vet caps on. We stood within the circle of prison buildings, in the center of concrete cell blocks, dining hall, classrooms, a hospital, a chapel. The grounds are brightly landscaped by the inmates, but the buildings look like a child's play structure that has been left outside for a hundred years—a plastic and castley hodgepodge of stone and concrete, ornate, crumbly, deteriorated.

There's razor wire everywhere, and a constant clanging and banging of gates and cells and doors. Guards carry arms, and keys that could be from the Middle Ages. Prisoners walk all over the grounds, as slowly as monks, with nowhere much to go. Of course, we saw your better inmates, the really polite ones, not the hard cases, not the men on death row. Those we saw and spent time with seemed to be sliding by, relatively seamless and calm. They're mostly older; you sense that their testosterone levels are down.

I like that in a prisoner.

Wolf and his friends showed us classrooms, the chapel, and the hobby shop where inmates work making wooden cable-car jewelry boxes and stained-glass hummingbirds and crosses. "Should you guys be trusted with knives and saws and extremely sharp implements?" I asked nicely.

They laughed. "We earned the privilege by good behavior," Wolf told me. He showed us the old dining hall with the long walls covered in murals done by inmates in black and brown shoe polish. The murals depicted California's history and their own—the Miwok on Mount Tamalpais, Sir Francis Drake on the beaches of West Marin, the Spanish missions, the Gold Rush, heroes of labor, farm workers, artists, prisoners, saints—and hidden inside the pictures were secrets only they could see.

We walked to the main cell block. The prison is over-crowded. The prisoners are double-celled, double-bunked. The cells are grotesque, like a Croatian zoo. I understand how the families of victims might think the prisoners deserve this, but seeing them stuffed in these cages affected me the same way seeing photos of the displayed corpses of Saddam Hussein's sons did. You had to wonder: Who are we? And what next? Bloody heads on stakes, outside the White House?

"What are you reading?" I asked a man in one cell.

He held out his book: true crime by Ann Rule.

Wolf led us to a dining hall, where sixty prisoners had gathered in bolted-down chairs near a stage. Behind them, a kitchen staff and prisoners were preparing the next meal, with guards nearby.

What you might call the aesthetics left something to be desired—an echoey, cavernous space, like a hangar, metallic, with the racket of people preparing food. It smelled like cheap meat and old oil and white bread.

I went onstage, took a long, deep breath, and wondered, as usual, where to start. I told the prisoners the

same things I tell people at writing conferences: Pay attention, take notes, give yourself short assignments, let yourself write shitty first drafts, ask people for help, and you
own what happens to you. They listened dutifully.

Then I introduced Neshama, with a concern that the
prisoners wouldn't quite get her—this intense grandmother with a nice big butt and fuzzy gray hair, wearing a
loud plaid flannel dress. I had invited her because I love
her stories and knew it would be more fun for me, and
because some people at San Quentin, like Neshama, hate
to write but love to read and tell stories.

I had extremely low expectations—I hoped a few prisoners might form a guild, like the one to which Neshama
belongs; I hoped they wouldn't hurt her, or overcome her,
or try to make her marry them. Neshama walked to the
mike and told her first story, her version of a folktale. It
was about a man with no luck, who comes upon safety,
wealth, and a beautiful woman, but is too busy looking
for fancier luck, somewhere else, to even notice her.
Neshama painted the story with her hands, leaning into
the crowd, and drawing back, hopeful or aghast at the
unlucky man's journey, smiling gleefully at the story's
close. And the place went nuts. She stole the show right
out from under me like a rock star, while I looked as prim

and mainstream as Laura Bush. Here they had thought Neshama was going to teach them a lesson, and she had instead sung them a song. Their faces lit up with surprise. She was shining on them, and they felt her shining on them, and so they shone back on her.

They asked her questions. Where do we find these stories? And Neshama told them: "They're in you, like jewels in your hearts." Why do they matter? "Because they're treasures. These memories, these images, come forth from the ground of the same wisdom we all know, but that you alone can tell."

The prisoners stared at her, mesmerized. They looked like family, and neighbors, black and white and Asian and Hispanic, all in their blue denim clothes. Some looked pissed off, some bored, some attentive; the older ones all looked like God.

When I at last got Neshama off the stage, I gave them a second round of my best writing tips. There was warm, respectful applause. Neshama got up and told a second story. It was about her late husband, and a pool he would hike to, where there was a single old whiskery fish swimming around. Neshama stripped her story down to its essence, because only essence speaks to desperate people. And the men rose to give her a standing ovation. It was a stunning moment. All she had done was tell them, "I'm human, you're human, let me greet your humanness. Let's be people together for a while."

Neshama explained to them about her storytelling guild, and one of the guards sat down to listen. We did a duet, the two of us answering questions, telling the men useful stories of our own work, and the writers we love, whom maybe they would love, too, who have filled our communal well, worn and honed from many years and different backgrounds.

We had evoked the listening child in these men, with the only real story anyone has ever told—that the teller has been alive for a certain number of years, and has learned a little in surprising ways, in the way the universe delivers truth. While I saw these men through the haze of our desire that things go well, I also saw beautiful rough glass, tumbled in the turbulent and unrelenting streams of prison life. I saw that these men looked out for one another. I saw that they had nothing but the present, the insides of their minds, glimpses of natural beauty, library books, guilt, rage, growth, and one another. I saw that these lives were of value. I had a sudden desire to send them all my books, all of my father's and friends' books, as well. Also to donate my organs. Why did these men make me feel like being so generous? Maybe it was all the fresh air we'd brought in, the wind and the rain and ourselves. It was as if we'd come with an accordion, and as we talked and listened, the bellows filled, and let breath, ours and theirs, in and out past the metal reeds.

fifteen

holding on

I am not sure how this happened, but Sam has become a young man, who needs to shave, who will be driving soon. Maybe I fed him too much. Thirteen was shocking enough, but compared with fourteen, it was training-wheels adolescence, a much cuter sullenness. Fourteen is hard-core, biker adolescence. He can be at a friend's for twenty-four hours, and has to check in only twice during that period. And yet, at the same time that he has grown seriously independent, with the ability to do some real damage to himself, I can still see the boy he has always been—inventive, playful, gangly—even as I can glimpse the man he is becoming. He's handsome, stylish, lean. He has great hair, and insists on getting haircuts in San Francisco now, instead of the twelve-dollar cuts down the street. He (mostly) has a good head on his shoulders and, just as important, a deep silliness, and decency. So now there's the sweet person he's always been, whom he'll still carry when he qualifies for senior admission prices, and there's the man he's becoming; but periodically, Phil stops by for a visit, the alien who has chosen Sam as a host body.

Phil is hairy and scary and awful. He was here yesterday. When I asked Sam to take his dishes to the sink, Phil slid into the space behind his eyes and looked at me with patronizing disbelief, as if he'd heard wrong—as if on a whim I had just asked him to go fetch some rock from the quarry for me.

I stared him down, and he backed down, and when Sam returned from the kitchen, Phil was gone.

Sam and I played with the dog and sat on the couch together for a while: I read, he drew. Later we went our separate ways. He went to *The Hulk* with his friends, and I went to a marvelous movie about a Maori girl, *Whale Rider*. He was home by eleven, his curfew, with two moosey pals who think I'm okay because I have dreads, and because they are not stuck with me.

We all got up at ten for church. Since Sam has to go to

church with me every two weeks, his friends often tag along. They don't hate church, because no one is making them go. They are actually all believers, too, cool guys who sometimes pray. One of them prayed with us when we were caught in a snowstorm on a ski trip. I know Sam believes that Jesus is true; sometimes he tells me about having prayed when he felt afraid, or he'll say jovially, "God is really showing off for us today." He makes fun of me for being a bit of a Jesus freak, but he loves a gold cross I gave him—referred to as his "bling," or even his "bling-bling"—and we often pray together at bedtime, especially if someone we love is having a hard time. Sam has a life that encompasses his own spirituality.

But he hates church.

Then why do I make him go? Because I want him to. We live in bewildering, drastic times, and a little spiritual guidance never killed anyone. I think it's a fair compromise that every other week he has to come to the place that has been the tap for me: I want him to see the people who loved me when I felt most unlovable, who have loved him since I first told them that I was pregnant, even though he might not want to be with them. I want him to see their faces. He gets the most valuable things I know through osmosis.

Also, he has no job, no car, no income. He needs to stay in my good graces.

While he lives at my house, he has to do things my way. And there are worse things for kids than to have to spend time with people who love God. Teenagers who do not go to church are adored by God, but they don't get to meet some of the people who love God back. Learning to love back is the hardest part of being alive. Besides, since Sam is the only teenager in his circle who has to go to church, I can't send him off to experience other churches or temples or mosques or Zen practice with his friends' families, because they don't go.

When I am trying to make decisions about what I hold most deeply in my heart, I am no longer in the land of reason and negotiation. While I can feel Sam's agonized resistance to attending church, I know there is nourishment for him there—there is real teaching—and a prime parental role is to insist that your kid get real teaching. Showing up is the lesson. The singing is the lesson, and the power of community. I can't get this to him in a nice package, like a toaster pastry or take-out. So every two weeks, I make him come to church with me.

I try to help it go down as easily as possible. We stop at McDonald's on the way there, we hang out at Best

Buy on the way home. Sam doesn't complain all that much. Maybe I've broken his spirit, my wild pony of Chincoteague.

When we got to church, he and his friends went to sit with the other teenagers, in the back. This is another reason I make him go: There is a youth group now, which meets every two weeks, in a room away from the grown-ups and the little kids. They lumber out of the service with their leader after the Passing of the Peace. The kids in the group get special snacks—cocoa and danish. Some might call this a bribe. I certainly would. I'm all for bribery when it's for a good cause. I think God does a lot of bait-and-switch. Peter catches a boatload of fish, then gets to become a disciple. We're herd animals, horse-people, and sometimes a bright orange carrot is the only thing that will get us to move.

I make Sam go because the youth-group leaders know things that I don't. They know what teenagers are looking for, and need—they need adults who have stayed alive and vital, adults they wouldn't mind growing up to be. And they need total acceptance of who they are, from adults they trust, and to be welcomed in whatever condition life has left them—needy, walled off. They want guides, adults who know how to act like adults but with a kid's heart. They want people who will sit with them and talk about the big questions, even if they don't have the answers; adults who won't correct their feelings or pretend not to be afraid. They are looking for adventure, experience, pilgrimages, and thrills. And then they want a home they can return to, where things are stable and welcoming. I mean, how crazy can you get?

Sam told one youth-group leader, Mark, that he knows instinctively that God wants him to have a life. That God would want him to surf and be alive and out having fun on a Sunday morning. That it's physically painful for him to sit indoors on a Sunday.

"Then why are you here?" Mark asked.

"Because my mother wants me here to share it with her," Sam said.

"I think that's a really good reason," Mark said.

I've seen Sam sneak glances at Mark. I know he wants what Mark has—not the faith part, necessarily, but the humor, the great vibe. ("Vibe is everything," Sam confided to me after a recent youth-group meeting with Mark.)

Most of the kids in the group came over to give me a hug during the Passing of the Peace. I was their Sunday-school teacher before they were teenagers, and they trust me: I helped Sunday school go down more easily for them. I loved them, gave them good snacks, drawing paper. I let them go outside for the Sacrament of the Lawn, to blow bubbles and play catch. Some of them have lost years and siblings to foster care and institutionalization. Some have lost parents to violence and addiction. Many have fallen through the cracks their whole lives—but not here, not on Sundays.

When Sam came over to hug me during the Passing of the Peace, it was like being hugged by the Frankenstein monster, but he let me smell his neck for a moment.

I half listened to the children's sermon; I thought mostly about the whales in *Whale Rider*. They're covered with clusters of barnacles the size of platters, all that stuff that attaches itself to whales because of its need, not the whales'. It's obviously good for the barnacles—it's a better ride, and they're bathed in nourishment, but I can't see how it might benefit the whales. I started thinking of my mother, as both whale and barnacle. In her last ten years, she lived on me. She couldn't help it; she wanted to stay alive, and I was her ride. Looking around at the faces of the people in my church, I could see their barnacles, too—all the usual old failures and sorrows, all the loss and ruckus of life that they have survived, excreted through the skin. Yet in *Whale Rider,* the barnacles are what the girl held on to like a saddle horn as she rode the whale. Without them, she couldn't have climbed on.

I watched Sam listen to the choir, fidgety, but he seemed to listen on and off. I listen to his horrible music all the time, so he can listen to the music I love every two weeks. It is raw and exquisite and subversive—you can tell that the singers will not be moved, except by the Spirit; they will not be nipped and tugged at by stupid details and lies. They know who they are—who we all are, one family on this earth—and they sing with their heels dug in, like kids who trust enough to fall backward into someone's arms.

After the song, the teens trudged off together, avoiding eye contact with the rest of us. They're distrustful and spiky—life is weird and doesn't deliver, and adults try to lead them like horses in the direction they think will make them happy, yet for the most part they won't go. But the teenagers can't make the congregation stop smiling at them; they can't make them stop singing, or blessing them.

I was glad for Sam when he went off with his peers and the group leader after the Peace. The youth group is much less embarrassing. Of course he doesn't want to come to regular worship—it's so naked, built on the rub-

ble of need and ruin, and our joy is deeply uncool—but
he doesn't want to floss or do homework either. He does
not want to have any hard work, ever, but I can't give him
that without injuring him. It's good to do uncomfortable
things. It's weight training for life.

He and his friends were in a good mood when church
ended, but then we had to drop the friends off at their
houses. They had things to do with their families, things
they really did not want to do. Sam was bored and com-
plaining when we got home. I made him lunch, and went
to bed with the cat and the Church of *The New York
Times*. When I woke up from a nap, I heard a commotion
in the living room. Sam had gathered a dozen of his
old stuffed animals and divided them into two warring
camps—the bunnies versus the bears. The bunnies were
inside a fortress of books, and a bear had been sent over
the walls with an exercise-band catapult. There were
great growling roars—very angry bunnies, bashing, wipe-
outs, beloved old animals gone bad. It was a ferocious
installation.

Sam let me watch. He called on his reserves of silliness
to break through, and reconnect, with his embarrassment
of a mother. Something made him willing to step off the
storm-tossed rocks, scowling and sinking, and hold on to

me, our home, his childhood, just as the Maori girl held on to the whale. What got her on the whale was her fierce understanding of her own truth, and that allowed her to tune into the whale's spirit, as the whale was tuned into hers. But she couldn't have held on without the barnacles on the whale's back—the barnacles to which I have clung when I was trying something bold and outrageous and impossible, like being a writer, or helping my parents die with dignity, or learning to love my increasingly bodily body. My inner sense of disfigurement, the unfairness of the world, all the stumbling blocks, the breakups, the bad news, and the things I was made to endure that I hated, these were what grew the barnacles.

Sam has come through so many trials, and has already tested me to the limits of my faith and patience—without even having gotten his driver's license yet. So while his current ride on earth is thrilling and important, what he has lived through and has been loved through is what helps him stay more or less balanced on the whale.

sixteen

one hand
clapping

On Father's Day two years ago, a bear of a man named Dwight, who does not have any children, spoke from the pulpit of my church about fatherhood. "I didn't learn about a father's love from my father," he said. "I learned about a father's love from my wife."

She was sitting in the front row. You couldn't miss her: she had only one hand.

This was a year after she and Dwight first started coming to our church, right after Anne had gone through treatment for breast cancer. She was brilliant, an activist and a passionate Christian, and I loved that she spoke from the heart about her own needs, and the world's

children, and the Bush crusade, without rehearsing—
because you don't have to rehearse the truth. But she
seemed too intense, and I wondered if perhaps she was
also a little cuckoo, which I suppose is not the politically
correct word. Anne sometimes sounded like a mad Old
Testament prophet, beseeching us to tend to the starving
people of the world, to save the rain forests. (Remember
the rain forests? Doesn't that seem a long time ago, those
stupid rain forests?)

She was so unabashed in her faithfulness and need
that it made some people nervous. Maybe I'm more comfortable with a little bashed, as the world leaves you feeling so often. When she really got going, she made the rest
of us seem positively staid. We'd be having a politely rous-
ing service, until this emaciated, freckled figure with
sparse baby-bird blond hair would start to rage against
Bush. She'd cry out about the suffering in the Third
World, and the evils of the military-industrial complex.
She waved her stump for emphasis, or testimony. She
waved it when she sang. She was like your craziest aunt,
the religious one with funny eyes who drinks.

Her pale skin was pink and raw in places, as if someone had tried to erase some of the freckles too roughly.

Initially, I tried to keep my distance and make her understand that she and I were more church family than friends, but she did not seem to get it, or simply would not obey. She brought me Mary mementos and Jesusy things to carry with me when I traveled, and she called me sometimes to ask how Sam and I were. But then she'd go too far—twice she cornered me after services, badgering me to show up at KPFA, the great left-wing radio station in Berkeley, to pray outside its doors: for peace, for the poor, for the earth. She insisted that people would listen to me because I was a writer. I had a voice, and I should use it to get Jesus' children cared for. I'll rant, I told her, and I'll get arrested, but I was not yet evolved enough to get down on my knees on the streets of Berkeley. I am just not a pray-at-KPFA kind of girl.

Once when I was heading out on a book tour, she foisted a heavy-hooded handmade monk's robe on me, straight out of *The Name of the Rose,* and suggested I wear it onstage to declare my love for Christ, and to ward off evil. I hid it in a closet at home—I have enough trouble wearing certain colors onstage, let alone a robe and cowl.

Little by little, though, I let her into my heart. True, she was odd, but she was also courageous, and dear, kind, and feisty, and very tender toward the children at church. I started sitting next to her during worship, sharing a hymnal or a Bible, and calling her at home from time to time to ask how she was. One day, on the phone, I asked about the stump, and she told me the story: Her mother had been a chemist for the military in World War II, helping develop chemical weapons. Several of her colleagues had also given birth to children with defects; her mother couldn't cope with Anne's. She was disgusted by the stump, and always positioned Anne so that it didn't show in family pictures.

Anne called it her paw.

One Sunday last year, during the Prayers of the People, Anne announced that her cancer had returned; she'd been given only a few months to live. She and Dwight had decided against any more chemo: they would trust God's grace and love to see her through.

She grew weaker and more emaciated, but when she could make it to church, she spoke and praised with more urgency, more need, and more gratitude for God's constant presence and mercy.

As the cancer progressed, she needed stronger pain medicine, and consequently her prayers grew longer and loopier. Her message was always the same, though: God loved the world, all evidence to the contrary, and we must not give up on God. The light shone in the darkness, and the darkness had not overcome it. She had Dwight, a cat, Jesus, and the members of our church, and very little scared her. She was a true believer.

I asked her to talk to my kids in church school about her faith, and one Sunday she came. The kids ranged in age from five years old to twelve. They all knew she was very sick. She asked each of them their names, and then whether they had noticed anything unusual about her. There was a polite silence. The children shook their heads with burlesque puzzled looks, until one kid all but smote his forehead, and said, "Oh! You mean the hand!" She nodded.

She let them examine the stump, up close. "Wow," said another kid. "Whatcha got there?"

She showed them the scar tissue where she'd had surgery as a baby to remove tiny vestigial fingers. The kids studied it with the fearless attention with which they might have examined a huge potato bug. She told them her story, of her mother's job as a military chemist, of the family pictures where other people's bodies hid her hand.

How she learned to pass as normal, as whole, to do so many amazing things that it took the attention off her body. "I was a good student, a terrific pianist. And such a good girl. But I was very lonely. My mother found me disgusting. And only a few people over the years wanted to hold my hand."

The children couldn't take their eyes off her, the weightless body, the strange paw. "The offer was that if I shared my mother's opinion of me, I got her. Otherwise I was totally alone. Until one day, Jesus came into the great emptiness."

It happened when Anne was six or so. She was sitting on her rocking chair in her bedroom, when she suddenly noticed a baby's face in the scar tissue. She wrapped the end of her arm in a scarf, swaddling it, so only the features in the scar tissue showed. "It looked like a doll," she told the children. "And it was looking at me very, very gently."

She invited the children to come close again and see the baby, which they all could make out, once they knew what to look for. "It was me," she said. "Both children were me. The six-year-old who was doing the mothering and the baby were both me. And I felt Jesus looking up at me, from inside the baby. And he was saying, 'I'm sorry it turned out this way, but you are whole in my eyes.' So I got me back, and in Jesus, I found a real mother."

"And how are you now?" I asked.

"I'm getting weak. Soon I'll be like a little child. I won't be able to walk, and I'll be totally dependent. But Dwight has promised to take care of me every step of the way. So at last I'm getting to have the earthly experience of being a small, cherished child."

"Did you mind having only one hand?" a girl asked.

"I didn't like it *at all*. It's been harrowing. And there are many things I love to do that I can't do well. I love making furniture, but it's too hard. I know there are other one-handed people who would hold the nails in their mouth and nail away, but I just can't do it. My lips would get bruised. And this one hand is always exhausted and banged up.

"Having this paw made me notice how much suffering there is in the world. It makes me ask, 'What's that suffering about? What's the answer?' The suffering itself means nothing. But the answer is also that I can't look away from it. I saw that God wanted me to help relieve the suffering. And that work has given me peace."

Anne came to church not long before she died. She

asked us to pray for Dwight and her as her life ended.
They both were teary but calm.

Dwight called me a few days later. Anne needed a
favor. She had asked the funeral home to deliver the box
in which her body would be carried away for cremation,
so she could get comfortable with this last piece of her
death, but it made her terribly afraid. She wanted the children from the church to decorate it for her.

This, of course, would have been too frightening for
them, so we asked the parents' permission, and when the
kids came to church the next Sunday, we commissioned
several dozen paintings. The kids painted angels, and
bridges to heaven, and cats waiting for Anne on the other
side. The little ones made hearts, and stick figures of
Jesus, cats, and Power Rangers; the older ones wrote messages beside their drawings, telling Anne not to be afraid.
The next day some of us grown-ups from church drove to
her house in the woods to paste the art onto her casket.
She was still alive, but barely, in a child-size nightie, sitting up in her bed in a room surrounded by trees, filled
with sun. We would take turns sitting on the bed with her,
singing, praying out loud. She was as stripped down to
nothing as you can be while still breathing, like a plant, or
a yogi, barely able to open her eyes, but she smiled a few

times. Dwight spent most of the time on the porch with the casket crew, pasting pictures, filling the empty spaces with calendar art, until the casket had been transformed into a gift box.

We had a memorial service for Anne on a Sunday soon after she died. We began with her favorite hymn, "Approach, My Soul, the Mercy Seat." Then Veronica spoke. She was exhausted from the morning service and her early-afternoon pastoral visits, but she reached into the empty well of herself and was visibly revived by the giving. She said that faith is not about how we feel; it is about how we live. And Anne lived her own eulogy, gardening, praising God, fighting the great good fight for justice, loving Dwight, playing piano, doing her yoga. Anne believed, without wavering. You don't run into such faithfulness often, faith in the goodness of the world.

A woman named Ranola got ready to sing a solo in the last hymn, "Near the Cross." She took a deep breath as she sat waiting, her eyes closed, with an air of quiet intensity. When Ranola opens her mouth to sing, she becomes a channel, raw and plain. The notes come from the Lord, who sings inside her. She opens her mouth and lets the Lord out. It's like calling from the mountains. When the choir rose, Ranola rose with them, her eyes still closed, and they all began to sway. You felt she could wait forever to begin. I looked off for a moment to the altar. There were vases of funeral flowers everywhere, gorgeous, purple-black, faded like daguerreotypes, flowers on their way to somewhere else, passing from one substance to another.

seventeen

◉

loving your president: day 2

Thank God for the fall. Summer nearly does me in every year. It's too hot, and the light is unforgiving, and the days go on way too long. And this year, the war on Iraq was raging. I felt soul-sick this summer to discover the secret gladness in me that the war was going so badly. I hated it about myself. I felt addicted to the energy of scorning my president. I thought that if people like me stopped hating him, it would mean that he had won.

Then summer turned to autumn.

I headed out for church one Sunday filled with my usual mix of joy and profound anxiety about life. But church is my favorite place on earth, after the couch in my living room. In church, we don't live from our minds—we live in community, which is to say, in shared loss and hope, singing, hanging out together. We don't sit huddled together, thinking.

I talked to more than one person before the service began, about the snap in the air. Everyone seemed glad summer was over. Spring is sweet, the baby season; summer is the teenage season—too much energy, too much growth and beauty and heat and late nights, none of them what they are cracked up to be. Fall is the older season, a more seasoned season. The weather surrounds you instead of beating down on you. Clouds bobble across the sky, and there are fresh winds, and misty salmon sunrises, and then cool blue skies. The weather is lighter, marbled, and it makes you feel like striding again, makes you glad that so much works at all.

There has been less light as the colors begin to change, and the world has grown more desperate.

Day 1 of this story begins one Sunday morning before church. It was overcast, and cold. I started cleaning out drawers, for no particular reason except that I had half an hour until I had to leave for church. In the back of one drawer, I found a horribly tangled gold chain. I took it

outside and sat down on the front step in the cool morning, and tugged on it. Tugging is what you always try first
with a tangled chain of slinky filament. It makes things
worse, but it's what you do.

I used to love to untangle chains when I was a child. I
had thin, busy fingers, and I never gave up. Perhaps
there was a psychiatric component to my concentration,
but as with much of my psychic damage, this worked to
everyone's advantage.

My mother might find a thin gold chain in a drawer,
wadded into an impossibly tight knot, and give it to me to
untangle. It would have a shiny, sweaty smell, and excite
me: gold chains linked you to the great fairy tales and
myths, to Arabia and India, to the great weight of the
world; yet they were light as a feather.

Sometimes I would put the chain on a table and work
it gently, letting the slink slip itself out of the knot, but
other times I had to use a needle to loosen the worst of it,
poking lightly so I wouldn't break any of the links.

Now, though, after a few minutes on the front step, I
went inside and put the chain back in the drawer, and sat
down to read the paper. This was a big mistake. Lately
our pastor had been urging us to act more like Martin

Luther King, Jr., which I feel gives an unfair advantage to the more decent and humane people. The rage returned in me.

I've known for years that resentments don't hurt the person we resent, but that they do hurt and even sometimes kill us. I'd been asking myself, Am I willing to try to give up a bit of this hatred?

Yeah; finally; theoretically. And that was a start.

I wondered whether I could try to love my president, as Jesus or Dr. King would, without having to want to have him over for lunch. But if you refused even to entertain the idea of eating lunch with the person in the distant future, would Jesus consider that you had really forgiven him?

Jesus ate with sinners—but of course, they ended up killing him. So there's that.

Still, I know he would eat with my president, even if he knew that the White House would probably call the police or the Justice Department on him later for his radical positions. He'd do it, because he is available to everyone. His love and mercy fall equally upon us all. This is so deeply not me. I *know* the world is loved by God, as are all of its people, but it is much easier to believe that God hates or disapproves of or punishes the same people

I do, because these thoughts are what is going on inside me much of the time.

◉

While singing in church that day, and while sitting in silent prayer and confession, I decided to experiment with change itself, as summer was turning to fall.

Unfortunately, change and forgiveness do not come easily for me, but *any* willingness to let go inevitably comes from pain; and the desire to change changes you, and jiggles the spirit, gets to it somehow, to the deepest, hardest, most ruined parts. And then Spirit expands, because that is its nature, and it drags along the body, and finally, the mind.

So when the seasons change, buckle up.

Everything was sweet at church, the singing, the kindness, and then the pastor had to go and ruin it all by giving a sermon on loving our enemies.

It was like being in the Twilight Zone.

It was clear that Veronica was speaking directly to me. She said that Christians have a very bad reputation in the world, and we have earned it, with our hate and self-righteousness. We speak in reverent terms of grace, justice, equality, mercy, and then we despise people who are also created in God's image, who are Her children, too. Veronica said that if the president had been the only person on earth, Jesus would still have loved him so much that he would have come down and died for him.

This drives me crazy, that God seems to have no taste, and no standards. Yet on most days, this is what gives some of us hope.

I sat there in church, working this through in my mind, tugging at it, yet hunkered down on the inside to protect myself from having to take it in, and then Veronica said one of the most stunning things I've heard her say: "When someone is acting *butt*-ugly, God loves them just the same as God loves the innocent. They are still just as loved by God." I was shocked. Boy, I thought, are you going to get it when Mom finds out that you said "butt" in church. I thought she was talking about the White House, but then she kept on about Jesus, and Dr. King, and—if you read between the lines—the people in our church. All of us—and there are some exquisitely good people in this church. It was outrageous. Veronica said you don't have to support people's political agendas, but you do have to love them, if you want to follow Jesus. She said you could tell if people were following Jesus, instead of following the people who follow Jesus, because they were feeding the poor, sharing their wealth, and trying to help everyone get medical insurance.

In my head I saw the president, marching on an aircraft carrier, with his little squinched-up Yertle the Turtle mouth, like a five-year-old whose dad owns the ship. Which his dad probably does. Then I saw him in a photo op, signing papers, and something made me stop. I wasn't thinking about his legislation or his tax cuts for the wealthy—I just experimented with the idea that God loves him just as much as God loves my niece Clara, that God looks at him in the same way my brother looks at baby Clara. How could this be? It didn't seem right. But I stuck with it. And after a while I could feel the tiniest of spaces in the knot, the lightest breath between tangled links. In that space, I saw the face of a boy I used to know superimposed on the president's face, a boy named John who liked the smartest girl in first grade. When she wrote at her desk, she squinched up her face fiercely, intently, and John thought that expression was what helped her to be so smart. So he squinched up his face, too, when he read, for the entire year.

For a few seconds, I imagined my president doing this in first grade as well. Actually, I *remembered* him doing this, about a week before, in the Oval Office. But then I imagined him as one of the people in my own family, who failed at school or in life, who got lost or bitchy or drunk, all that innate beauty getting fucked up. As mine did.

To be honest, I am never going to get anywhere with this president. But Jesus kept harping on forgiveness and loving one's enemies, so I decided to try. Why couldn't Jesus command us to obsess about everything, to try to control and manipulate people, to try not to breathe at all, or to pay attention, stomp away to brood when people annoy us, and then eat a big bag of Hershey's Kisses in bed?

Maybe in some translations, he does.

The sermon ended; people were crying. Veronica asked if anyone wanted to come forward for special prayer. Apparently no one did. I struggled to keep in my seat, but I found myself standing, then lurching forward stiffly. Veronica asked me quietly what I needed, and I whispered that I was so angry with and afraid of the right wing in this country that it was making me mentally ill. She put her arm around me, and the church prayed for me, although they did not know what was wrong.

I felt a shift inside, the conviction that love was having its way with me, softening me, changing my cold stone heart. The feeling grew stronger and stronger, until, unfortunately, church was over.

Driving home, I tried to hold on to what I'd heard that day: that loving your enemies was nonnegotiable. It meant trying to respect them, it meant identifying with their humanity and weaknesses. It didn't mean unconditional acceptance of their crazy behavior. They were still accountable for the atrocities they'd perpetrated, as you were accountable for yours. But you worked at doing better, at loving them, for the profoundest spiritual reason: You were trying not to make things worse.

Day 1 went pretty well. All things considered.

I e-mailed Veronica that night, and I said that I'd heard her, way deep down. I didn't know how it would change my behavior, but I had heard. She answered that this was a powerful beginning, to hear the truth, and to tell the truth. We don't transform ourselves, she said, but when we finally hear, the Spirit has access to our hearts, and that is what changes us.

I lay in the dark and thought about this brief but amazing moment in church. It had felt almost like the moment when I converted, and later when I got sober, a baby sense of hope, a chance of release from the constant knots in my stomach. I had poked a needle into another knot that day, tugged, let go, and finally felt some give. It was more tenuous than with a metal chain, with which, if you stay with it, you have something to show at the end— gold! And as with any chain, when you get anywhere, you should hang it up or put it on immediately, instead of let- ting it lie around, because the tangle is waiting to happen again. So I sang silent songs to myself until I fell asleep.

I have to admit it, though: Day 2 was a bit of a dis- appointment.

It began well enough, with a molten autumn sunrise, and ended with a silver moon. But the hours in between did not go nearly as well as I had been hoping. I was fine, until I heard the latest bad news from Iraq, and my hos- tilities flared up again. It continues to be a struggle. I know that God is in the struggle with us. And that trying to love the people in this White House is the single most subversive position I could take.

I got the chain out of the drawer and gave it another try, but I didn't have any patience. It crossed my mind to take a hammer to the miserable thing and bust it into pieces. Trying to unravel it was a waste of time. I didn't need it. But something inside me got back to work. Maybe I would find the perfect person to give it to—

someone who was down in the dumps, who'd lost all hope of change, whose spirits would be lifted by a little present. So, tug tug, poke poke: I have to believe that if I do this, it will cause change—there will be more give, and give means there is more light between the links. You never know exactly where the knot is going to release, but usually, if you keep working with it, it will.

◉

eighteen

scattering the
present

Most of me was glad when my mother died. She was a handful, but not in a cute way. More in a life-threatening way, that had caused me a long time ago to abandon all hope of ever feeling good about having had her as a mother. She was a mix of wrathful Old Testament opinion, terrified politeness and befuddled English arrogance—Hermione Gingold meets the dark Hindu goddess Kali. And God, she was annoying. I mean this objectively. You can ask my brothers, or her sister. I used to develop tics in her presence. Yet most of who I have become is the result of having had her as a foil, and having her inside me: as DNA, as memory; as all the weird lessons she taught, and the beautiful lessons, too—and they are the same.

While she was alive, I spent my life like a bitter bellhop, helping my mother carry around her psychic trunks. So a great load was lifted when she died, and my life became much easier. For a long while, I did not miss her at all, and did not forgive her a thing. I was the angriest daughter on earth, and also one of the most devoted. My brothers and I gave away most of her things—clothes, books, broken junk. One thing was left behind, and this was the plastic crematory box, with her misspelled name, that held her ashes. We couldn't figure out how to pry it open. In the many months it had taken me to retrieve the box from the closet, I discovered that I had forgiven her for a number of things, although for none of the big-ticket items—like having existed at all, for instance, and then having lived so long. Still, the mosaic chips of forgiveness I felt that day were a start. After I carried the box of ashes from the closet, wrapped it in pretty paper, and placed it on a shelf in my living room, a few more months passed before I felt like doing anything further. This is what happened next:

Around that time, Veronica gave a sermon about how, with the war raging in Iraq, now was not the time to figure everything out—for instance who was to blame. It was not the time to get a new plan together and try to push it through. It was time to be still, to center ourselves, to trust what we'd always trusted in: friendship, kindness, helping the poor, feeding the hungry. Having felt scattered for much of the past two years, I took Veronica's words to heart, and began to get quiet whenever possible, to take longer walks, to sit in beggy prayer and fretful meditation. My mind kept thinking its harsh thinky thoughts, but I would distract myself from them gently and say, "Those are not the truth, those are not trustworthy, those are for entertainment purposes only." Eventually I had quieter thoughts about my mother, to see her through what the theologian Howard Thurman called "quiet eyes." Not totally quiet eyes, in my case. But quiet for me, and then quieter still.

Gerald May wrote, "Grace threatens all my normalities." I tell you. It had taken two years for me to bring her out of the dark closet. Now I felt it was time to scatter her ashes with the family, to honor her. The problem was, I didn't honor her. I meant to, but all I really felt was sorry for how hard her life had been, and glad that she had finally passed. This is what the elders of our church call dying—passing, as in acing her exams, or turning down the offer to renew her lease. "Oh, yeah, she passed," they reassure you, and theologically, I believe, they are right on both counts.

That was where I was when Veronica urged us to be still. And when I did, I found out once again how flexible and wily the human spirit is. It will sneak out from behind the bushes like a cartoon cat and ambush you if you're not careful, trick you into giving up a teaspoon of resentment, get you to take one step back from the frozen ground. Mine was lying in wait for me the day I found a photograph of my mother when she was sixty, and while my heart didn't leap, it hopped, awkwardly, as if its shoelaces were tied together.

In the photo, she is wearing her usual heavy makeup, which I have always believed was a way of maintaining both disguise and surface tension; it always humiliated me. But in this one picture, instead of feeling humiliated, I could finally see what she was shooting for: to appear beautiful, and worthy, a vigorous woman on this earth. She is posing in front of a vase of flowers, clasping one wrist with her hand, as if trying to take her own pulse. She had been divorced for eight years or so by then. One of her eyebrows is arched, archly, as if one of her children had once again uttered something dubious or socially unacceptable. One-third of her is in darkness, two-thirds in light, which pretty much says it.

You can see what a brave little engine she was, even though she'd lost everything over the years—her husband, her career, her health. But she still had her friends and family, and she stayed fiercely loyal to liberal causes, and to underdogs. And I thought, Well, I honor that, so we'll start there.

The next thing I knew, I had called my relatives, most of whom still live in the Bay Area, where we all grew up, and had invited them to dinner on my mom and her twin's birthday, to scatter her ashes. Those ashes of hers were up against a lot—our lives were better since her death—but I believed that if we released her, this would release us, and she could release herself. Or I would have a complete breakdown and start to drink again, and Sam and I would have to go live at the rescue mission. I knew only that scattering her ashes was the next right thing.

Two weeks later, three aunts, an uncle, half a dozen cousins, my brother and sister-in-law, a six-year-old second cousin, and a friend came to dinner at my house. I adore these people. I have also had fights with some of them over the years, have said terrible things, have been accused by one of great wrongs, and told I would never

be forgiven. We've had the usual problems: failed mar-
riages, rehab, old resentments, miserable lumpy family
secrets, harshness and intensity. But we have loved and
cared for one another over the years. We're just another
motley American family, enduring. As my friend Neshama's
father-in-law used to say, looking around on holidays and
shaking his head, "We are a bum outfit."

After dinner, we hiked up the hill to the open space
near the house. One of my aunts, who says to say she is
fifty-four, totters when she walks now, and needs arms to
hold on to. Dallas, my six-year-old cousin, glommed on
to Sam, who dragged him along like carry-on luggage,
rolling his eyes but pleased. The wind was blowing, and
the sun was starting to go down. Sam and Dallas tore to
the top of the hill, while the rest of us, blown and buffeted
by the wind, took one another's arms, and walked in an
unsteady procession the rest of the way.

The sun was setting behind a ghost cloud, illuminating
it, imposing a circle of light over it, like a cookie cutter.
Eucalyptus trees circled around us, at the edge of the
grass, as if holding down the earth, bricks on a picnic
tablecloth in the wind. The trees were the only things
between us and the horizon. We could see 360 degrees
above fleecy trees, golden hillsides, towns. The wind

made us feel more exposed than usual: it was so gritty that it flayed us—but lucky us, someone pointed out, with bodies to be assailed.

Dallas tore around the periphery having goof attacks, flirting with Sam. "Does anyone want to see my fireworks?" he kept calling out. "Will anyone come and see them?"

"When we're done," his mother told him sternly. "Now leave us alone."

We stood in a circle for a few minutes. "I knew that if I asked you to come tonight, you would," I said. We all cried a little. My cousins had really loved my mother. She had a sweet voice, one of them said, and was always kind to them. My aunt Gertrud said, "The nature of life is harsh, and Nikki got some terrible breaks. It wasn't fair how things turned out for her. But she did a lot of good in her life, and we will always miss her."

"Yes, we will," a couple of people responded, the way we do at church. My heart was heavy with missing her, even as I felt the old familiar despair that she had been my mother. I just tried to breathe.

The reason I never give up hope is that everything is basically hopeless. Hopelessness underscores everything—the deep sadness and fear at the center of life, the holes in the heart of our families, the animal confusion within us. When you do give up hope, a lot can happen. When it's not pinned wriggling onto a shiny image or expectation, it may float forth and open like those fluted Japanese blossoms, flimsy and spastic, bright and warm. This almost always seems to happen in community: with family, related by blood, or chosen; at church, for me; at peace marches.

Then my brother Stevo walked a few dozen feet away from where we stood, and began to pry open the plastic box with a knife. "Want to see my fireworks?" Dallas cried, and his mother shushed him again. He raced about on the hillside. It was distracting, like having a puppy in church, but the setting sun defused my annoyance, and I remembered C. S. Lewis's observation: "We do not truly see light, we only see slower things lit by it." Except for Dallas, we were as big and slow as animals at a watering hole. We watched Stevo take out the bag of ashes and open it into the wind. He flung her away from the sunset, and the wind caught her and whooshed her away. Some of the ashes blew back onto my brother, and onto Gertrud, who stood beside him, scattering flowers into the plume. Ashes always stick and pester you long after you have scattered them: my brother looked as if he'd been cleaning a fireplace.

Then Dallas called out again, "Want to see my fireworks now? Doesn't anyone want to see my fireworks?" We all turned back toward the sun, where he stood, and gave him the go-ahead. He reached into his pockets, withdrawing fists full of something, and, looking at us roguishly, flung whatever he held up into the air. It turned out to be tiny pebbles, but he tossed with such ferocious velocity, as high as he could manage in the wind, that when they rained back down on us in the very last of the sun, they shone.

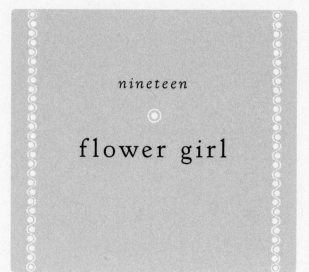

nineteen

flower girl

These are such rich, ripe times for paranoia and despair that each celebration, each occasion of tribal love and music and overeating glows more brightly against the swampy backdrop of the war in Iraq. I have never been more paranoid in my life—some days I'm like the comedian Emo Philips, who thought the man hammering on the roof next door was calling him a paranoid little weirdo, in Morse code. But I see people rising up, resisting, gearing up for another fight for decency, for freedom, for the poor, for the earth. And beating back the right wing's fever dream is going to be one of the all-time great fights. People are helping one another keep their spirits up. Great movies are being made, brilliant columns continue to be written, and wonderful art is being created, poetry, histories, edgy comedy, and theater. Along with the paranoia, I feel some hope. It didn't hurt that I recently served as a flower girl in a friend's wedding.

The bride and her parents are among my closest friends. I adore her, and so of course I wanted to be the best flower girl, creating a path of breathy joy upon which she might walk—the evanescence of rose petals, the sweetness. But there were a couple of problems: there were two other flower girls, one eight years old and the other three.

At first I could see no reason to have two little girls there to rain on my parade. Then I had a moment of clarity: It was not my parade.

I'd wanted to be an Herbal Essences shampoo vision, someone in a flowing dress with a garland in her hair. Someone who looked as if she should be accompanied by a unicorn. Instead, alongside those two young girls, I was going to look like Woody Allen in *Zelig*.

There was only one other woman in the bridal party, besides the bride—her sister, the maid of honor, who was the mother of the three-year-old. She had chosen a gauzy dress of heathery rose, flowing but deceptively tailored— in other words, you had to be thin to wear it. I know this because the bride asked me to try it on in my size at the vintage-style bridal store where the maid of honor had found her dress. I did, and I could barely get into it. Even the next-larger size hurt, like tight panty hose. I slunk away.

I called the bride and said the dress was hopeless. She said to look for something from the same designer, and suggested I make an appointment with the store manager, who is hip and helpful. I did.

The morning of my appointment, I tried to keep my perspective. Building a wedding is a recipe for muddle— the bridal party, the families, the guests, the minister, the vows, the food. You're attempting to make something beautiful out of unruly and unpredictable elements—the weather, the nuttier relatives, the rivalries, disorders, and dreams. Out of mostly old neurotic family and friends, you hope to create something harmonious. You do so as an act of faith, hoping that for a brief period of time, the love and commitment of two people will unite everyone; and it will sort of work. Even if the weather or personalities are worrisome, the breezes and water will flow through the structure of your wedding, will sanctify and change it, and it will hold.

I went to my appointment with the store manager. She was very nice. Perhaps a bit thin. Still, I thought of her as my caseworker. I told her that even the larger size of the heathery rose dress had been tight. "Oh," she exclaimed, "this line runs really small! You could try on the extra-large." I am not overweight; I used to be five-foot-seven, before I became a victim of what my son calls the old-age shrinking thing. Now I am five-foot-six, and weigh around 140. So let's say medium. Or let's remember the bumper sticker with the picture of the cat that says, "I'm not fat—I'm fluffy." I'm a little fluffy in the stomach now, and in the butt. So with the caseworker continuing to cry out that the line ran small, I tried on the extra-large, and it was hideous.

I felt despondent for caring. I am a feminist and a progressive—I'm sure I'm on the attorney general's enemies list. At any rate, he's on mine. I prayed for sanity and militant self-love to return—normally I'm just an ordinary American woman, still vulnerable enough after a lifetime of brainwashing to compare myself miserably with the fourteen-year-old models in magazines who are made up to look like twenty-year-olds. But now I was comparing myself unfavorably with an eight-year-old and a three-year-old.

This was not a bridal issue anymore, or even a fashion issue. It was a psychiatric issue.

I announced to my caseworker that this dress would not work in any circumstance, in any situation, like Sam-I-am in *Green Eggs and Ham*: I would not wear it on a boat, with a goat, with a turtle, in a girdle. My caseworker understood, and said we would find another dress from the same line as the maid of honor's. I tried on everything, and finally found a two-piece outfit by the same designer that you could buy in separate sizes—a medium blouse, say, and an extra-large skirt. I looked fine in the store, even pretty.

When I tried them on at home, however, I nearly fainted. I looked like Dame Edna. I called the bride to say I had to return the outfit, and would drop out of the wedding party. But she'd seen the outfit, at the store, and loved it.

I had a stern talk with myself, about getting out of myself to be a person for others, for the bride and her family. But after that, it was all downhill. There was the matter of the shoes, the unhappy details of which I will spare you, except to say that it was a total fucking nightmare. I went to six different stores on three different days before I found wine-colored Mary Janes with sexy, slutty crossover straps. They were the sort of shoes Courtney Love would have worn to a wedding in her Hole days, and they would go with the outfit, if I tore it, and wore lots of smeary red lipstick.

Everyone in the family was more joyful and excited and anxious as the wedding day approached. That's what's so touching about weddings: Two people fall in love, and decide to see if their love might stand up over time, if there might be enough grace and forgiveness and memory lapses to help the whole shebang hang together. Yet there is also much discomfort, and expense, and your hope is that on the big day, energy will run through the lightest elements and the heaviest, the brightest and the dullest, the funniest and the most annoying, and that the whole range will converge in a ring of celebration.

At the rehearsal the night before the wedding, we all met at the chapel—the bride and the groom, the father of the bride, the priest, the maid of honor, and her three-year-old daughter. The eight-year-old flower girl could not be there, and she did not really need to be, because there is no one more capable and helpful than an eight-year-old girl. The rehearsal went without a hitch, as long as the maid of honor was holding her daughter. But when she put her down momentarily, the three-year-old just sort of lost her mind. So for the rest of the rehearsal, her mother held her, and we got through it. It was actually a lot of fun.

On the ride home that night with the priest, I bleated out the question that had been on perhaps all our minds: What would we do if the little flower girl melted down during the actual wedding?

"Is it wrong to sedate children before they perform in a ceremony?" I asked. "To give them the merest hint of sacramental wine? Or Klonopin?"

The priest laughed. We drove along. I imagined the girl having a tantrum. I saw myself make threatening gestures at her with my fist.

Here's what the priest said: "I promise you it will all work out, in its own perfectly imperfect way. Weddings are about families, and families can be a bit of a mess under stress. But the love that will gather tomorrow night is much more important than anything else on earth, and bigger than anything else on earth, too. Because finally, that love is sovereign."

The next morning, I got my fingernails painted. The backs of my hands have had dark brown spots for years. The first time I showed them to my dermatologist, I thought they were melanomas. "They're probably what we used to call liver spots when I was younger," I said jocularly. He peered at them. "We still call them liver spots," he said. For the wedding, I wanted pretty pink nail polish to distract from them. I had my toenails painted as well. Not to brag, but I happen to have nice feet. They weren't even going to show, but I would know that my pink toenails inside my pretty red shoes were leading the way. They were like my inside three-year-old. You celebrate what works and you take tender care of what doesn't, with lotion, polish, and kindness.

Before leaving for the wedding, I smoothed on lots of lotion, a little makeup, my petit-four outfit, my red shoes. I tucked a lipstick and a bag of peanut M&M's into my purse, and left for the church with my boyfriend.

The other flower girls looked angelic, and miraculously, the eight-year-old had complete dominion over the three-year-old. The women hung out together in a room near the back entrance to the chapel—the bride, her mother and her sister, her two best friends, and the flower girls. The three-year-old clutched the eight-year-old, would not let her go, stared at her adoringly. I handed out M&M's and told everyone they were tranquilizers. I didn't feel any age, just giddy with surprise at the paradox that I may have looked old on the outside but felt so young on the inside. It's almost everyone's secret— we look in the mirror, saying, "Who is that old person?" while inside there's pretty much the same person we always were. A lot of stuff falls off—your vision, your youth, your memory—but better stuff is left behind.

When the processional was to begin, the three-year-old panicked, as expected, and my heart sank to see her look around desperately for her mother. She cried out her mother's name, but only once. "Shhh, shhh," I said, "let's go, darlings." The eight-year-old took her hand. There was a moment's pause. Then they began to march along together, and I fell into step beside them, and we tossed those translucent petals into the air.

twenty

◉

sam's brother

I got pregnant during Advent fifteen years ago, after which I had almost no further contact with Sam's father, John, for years. Who could have imagined that over the last seven years the three of us would become a quirky, tender family? Last week Sam and I went to visit his father in Canada for the fourth time. We came back home on the first Sunday in Advent.

This time Sam was going to meet his half brother, his father's first son, who is forty. No one had been ready to take this step until this year, and suddenly we all were. Sam was more excited than I'd seen him in a long time. I was, too, but—well, you know me with my bad nerves.

John's son was going to be staying on John's marvelous boat with his wife and baby. Sam would stay with John at his apartment, and I had booked a hotel with room service and cable TV, as I had not completely lost my mind.

John picked Sam and me up at the airport, took us out for sushi, and dropped me at my hotel. They headed off to John's apartment. My hotel was on the shore of an inlet that flows into Vancouver, with snowy mountain peaks across the water, trees seemingly aflame on every hillside, and a bustling harbor beneath my window. I was going to take a cab to John's later, and we would all meet up for dinner.

I holed up in my room with CNN and Kit Kats from the mini-bar, and grew increasingly tense. What if Sam's brother couldn't reach out, what if Sam went into adolescent glower mode, what if . . . I imagined everything that could go wrong that night, and then moved into the more spacious realms of gum surgery and colon cancer. I got some communion Milanos out of the mini-bar, performed the sacrament, and then prayed that I could just keep the faith. I have a lot of faith. But I am also afraid a lot, and have no real certainty about anything. I remembered something Father Tom had told me—that the opposite of faith is not doubt, but certainty. Certainty is missing the point entirely. Faith includes noticing the mess, the emptiness and discomfort, and letting it be there until some light returns. Faith also means reaching deeply within, for the sense one was born with, the sense, for example, to go for a walk.

First I showered off that horrible butt smell you get from being on an airplane. Then I bundled up and went outside. I prayed that everything would go all right, for Sam's sake. I wish faith wrapped you in a bubble, but it doesn't, not for long.

During Advent, Christians prepare for the birth of Jesus, which means the true light. All your better religions have a holy season as the days grow shorter, when we ask ourselves, Where is the spring? Will it actually come again this year, break through the quagmire, the terror, the cluelessness? Probably not, is my response, when I'm left to my own devices. All I can do is stay close to God, and my friends. I notice the darkness, light a few candles, scatter some seeds. And in Nature, and in my spiritual community, I can usually remember that we have to dread things only one day at a time. Insight doesn't help here. Hope is not logical. It always comes as a surprise, just when you think all hope is lost. Hope is the cousin to grief, and both take time: you can't short-circuit grief, or emptiness, and you can't patch it up with your bicycle tire tube kit. You have to take the next right action. Jesus would pray on the mountain, or hang out with the poor or the imprisoned, or—as I'll get to in a moment—start doodling in the sand.

I walked around town for a while, stopped at some bookstores, bought myself a lipstick, a cup of cocoa with extra whipped cream, and then dropped by an old stone church.

The church was small and beautiful, cold and dark. This gave me some relief: we live in darkness. People know this by the time they turn twenty-one; if they don't, they're seriously disturbed. I started to get freaked out about dinner—there are six people in the world with whom I can bear to eat. And besides, what if the added weight of Sam's brother, with his inevitable baggage, caused Sam's life and mine with John to buckle and collapse?

What if Sam's heart got broken again? As with most kids who are fourteen, it has been spackled and duct-taped and caulked back together many times as it is.

The church smelled dank and musky, like Sam's dirty laundry, but I sat quietly. My mind perched on top of my head like a spider monkey and thought of more things that could go wrong at dinner, and whose fault those things would be. I tried to drop my attention from my head to my heart, which is actually an ascension of sorts. My heart is so amazed that John and I have made a little family for Sam. Still, my mind chattered on, as if the spider monkey had taken acid. My mind is my main problem almost all the time. I wish I could leave it in the fridge when I go out, but it likes to come with me. I have tried to get it to take up a nice hobby, like macramé, but it prefers to think about things, and jot down what annoys it.

Another problem involves what I think the light looks like. I have thought, over the years, that the light would look like success, a good man, a child, a Democratic president, but none of these was right. Moses led his people in circles for forty years so they could get ready for the Promised Land, because they had too many ideas and preconceptions about what a Promised Land should look like. During Advent, we have to sit in our own anxiety and funkiness long enough to know what a Promised Land would be like, or, to put it another way, what it means to be saved—which, if we are to believe Jesus or Gandhi, specifically means to see everyone on earth as family.

I left the church and took a cab to John's. I cannot tell the whole story, but Sam says that I can share the following brief report: His brother is tall and warm. They looked enough alike that I could see they were related, but not so much that I had to breathe into a brown paper bag. And they were both a little shy. Sam's brother's wife is smart and lively, and their baby is lovely beyond words. We connected, in the perfectly imperfect way of families. We ate and were kind to one another. We watched TV and raced around after the baby. Sam staked out turf close to both me and his father, and ventured out as small children do to try new lines of conversation. I was hoping that something dramatic would happen, and I'd have a great story to tell, but after several hours I realized that this is the best story there is: A small group of related people came together, willing to be supremely uncomfortable, so that Sam could know his brother, and his brother's family, and therefore come to know a bit more about who he is. This is why we did it.

I am also allowed to report that Sam's niece and my niece Clara were born on the exact same day—I tell you, when God is not being cryptic and silent, He or She is so obvious. Sam was wonderful with his niece that day, like a cross between Big Bird and Tony Soprano. "Hey, you," he called to her, when she was babbling incoherently over the sound from his TV show, "put a sock in it." Then he performed the two most important functions for an uncle—made farting sounds to amuse her, and took care that she didn't get her fingers caught in any drawers.

Sam also doodled throughout the evening. The rest of us talked, overate, cleaned up messes as we went, held our tongues, ignored the inevitable family tension. The oil of manners made it possible. When you're kind to people, and you pay attention, you make a field of comfort around them, and you get it back—the Golden Rule meets the Law of Karma meets Murphy's Law.

And all the while, Sam drew his little guys, from time to time asserting his adolescent grump. I felt anxious much of time, but what else is new? Something larger than we were, larger than our anxieties and ferocious need to control, got us through, connected us, even if the connection was precarious at first. What shone through was the odd responsibility we took for one another, the kindness, marbled through the past, the bad and silent patches of our shared histories, our character defects, hidden and on the surface, and the glitches. Things got broken—they always do—and children always yap and stamp and cry and demand your attention. It's called real life, and it's cracked and fragile, but the glue for me is the beating of my heart, love, and whatever attention I can pay to what matters most to me—making a good life for Sam.

"Hey, Sam," I said, as I hugged everyone good-bye before leaving the hotel. "Doodle on."

◉

The next morning, I lay in bed giving thanks for having come from where we were before Sam knew his dad to where we were now. I ordered room service, and then made the mistake of turning on the TV. What if there really was no hope this time? What if the insanity had grown more intense than wisdom? Outside my window, the nearest trees looked sick and in trouble. Their leaves had all fallen, and they looked dead. I could only lean on my shaky Advent faith that things would be okay, more or less, that we are connected, and that everyone—everyone—eventually falls into the hands of God. I pray, and try to be kind, and go to church, and Sam doodles.

But these are the things that Jesus did, too. In John 8, when the woman is about to be stoned by the Pharisees for adultery, we see Jesus doodling in the sand. The Pharisees, the officially good people, are acting well within the law when they condemn the woman to death. A huge crowd of people willing to kill her joins them. The Greatest Hits moment here comes when Jesus challenges the crowd: "Let him who is without sin cast the first stone." But the more interesting stuff happens before, when he leaves the gathering storm, goes off by himself, and starts doodling.

Jesus refuses to interact with the people on their level of hatred and madness. He draws in the sand for a time. Maybe he's drawing his little guys—the Gospel doesn't say. But when he finally faces the mob and responds, all the people who were going to kill the woman have disappeared.

You have to wonder: Where was the man with whom she committed adultery? Some people suggest he is in the crowd, waiting to join in with the others and kill her. We don't know. But I can guess how the condemned woman must have felt—surprised. She was supposed to die, and her life was spared. Hope always catches us by surprise.

It poured all morning. Even in the gloom and desperation, I played over the scenes from the night before, in all their magic and klutziness and ordinariness: Sam and his brother getting to know each other; the baby in a state of busy wonder. I have to say, I continue to be deeply surprised by life.

I had invited everyone over to my hotel for room service lunch and a movie. I was anxious while I waited. The rain came down, dark and loud. I couldn't wait to get back to my own home: this was the perfect time to plant bulbs and scatter seeds, in the hope that some would grow. But meanwhile, in Advent, we show up when we are needed; we try to help, we prepare for an end to the despair. And we do this together.

twenty-one

○

falling better

Last year I was invited to Park City, Utah, to give some lectures just after Easter, and I scammed a free ski week out of the deal. Sam invited his friend Tony, and I invited my friend Sue Schuler. She was a great companion, younger than I but already wise; cheeky, gentle, blonde, full of life—and jaundiced, emaciated, dying of cancer.

She said yes. She had always loved to ski, and was a graceful daredevil on the slopes. I started skiing only six years ago, and tend to have balance and steering problems. I fall fairly often, and flounder getting up, but I enjoy the part between the spills, humiliations, and abject despair—sort of like real life.

No one in Sue's family, including Sue herself, was sure whether she'd be able to ski, or whether she would make the trip at all. But I was. No one could have known that she would die only one month after my invitation. I thought that if she saw those Wasatch Mountains, she'd at least want to try. I invited her because otherwise I was never going to see her again—she had cancer of the everything by then—and because she was distraught on Easter when I called to say hello. I felt she ought to have one last great Easter before she died. That would make up for a lot. Easter is so profound. Christmas was an afterthought in the early Church, the birth not observed for a few hundred years. But no one could help noticing the resurrection: "Spring is Christ," Rumi said, "martyred plants rising up from their shrouds." Easter says that love is more powerful than death; bigger than the dark, bigger than cancer, bigger than airport security lines.

Sue said yes, she'd meet me in Park City.

I'd met her about a year before, over the phone, through her sister, an old friend of mine. Barb was a sort of matchmaker, who recognized kindred souls in me and Sue, believers who loved to laugh. Barb had known me when I walked my friend Pammy through her last year of life. Call me crazy, but I did not immediately want to be friends with another dying blonde babe just then. But I felt God's hand in this, or at any rate, God's fingers on the Rolodex, flipping through names to find a last-ditch, funny, left-wing Christian friend for Sue.

It was March 2001. The wildflowers weren't in bloom yet; the bulbs hadn't opened. A month before she called me for the first time, Sue had been told that tumors had developed in her liver and lungs. She had been in a deep depression for a while, but she finally followed Barb's advice to call me after various people at her church kept saying that she could be happy—she was going home to be with Jesus. This is the type of thing that gives Christians a bad name. This, and the Inquisition. Sue wanted to open fire on them all. I think I encouraged this.

Some of her evangelical friends had insisted sorrowfully that her nieces wouldn't get into heaven, since they were Jews, as was one of her sisters. I told her what I believe to be true—that there was not one chance in a million that the nieces wouldn't go to heaven, and if I was wrong, who would even want to go? I promised that if there was any problem, she and I would refuse to go. We'd organize.

"What kind of shitty heaven would that be, anyway?" she asked.

That was the beginning of our friendship, which unfolded over a year and some change, a rich condensed broth of affection and loyalty, because there was no time to lose. I couldn't believe how beautiful Sue was when we met face to face: I hadn't expected that earthy, dark irreverence to belong to such a beauty. She started coming to my church soon after, and we talked on the phone regularly. I had one thing to offer, which is that I would just listen. I did not try to convince her that she could mount one more offensive against the metastases. I could hear her, hear the fear, and her spirit. Sue had called on New Year's Day 2002 in tears, to say she knew she was dying.

I listened for a long time; she went from crushed to defiant. "I have what *everyone* wants," she said. "But no one would be willing to pay."

"What do you have?"

"The two most important things. I got forced into loving myself. And I'm not afraid of dying anymore."

She got sicker and sicker. It was unfair—I wanted to file a report with the Commission on Fairness; and I still want to ask God about this when we meet. That someone so lovely and smart and fabulous was going to die, and that horrible people, whom I will not name, would live forever—it broke your heart. At the same time, she had so much joy. She loved her family, her friends, and eating. She ate like a horse. I have never known a woman who could put it away like Sue. Her body was stick-thin, and on top of that, the skin on one leg was reptilian, with twenty-two skin grafts from her knees up past her hips, which she'd needed upon contracting a flesh-eating disease at a hospital after one of her countless cancer surgeries.

I ask you.

This business of having been issued a body is deeply confusing—it's another thing I'd like to bring up with God. Bodies are so messy, and disappointing. Every time I see the bumper sticker that says, "We think we're humans having spiritual experiences, but we're really spirits, having human experiences," (a) I think it's true, and (b) I want to ram the car.

Sue and I met one last time on the Thursday after Easter 2002 in Park City, to celebrate the holiday privately, a week late. We shared a king-size bed in the condominium. Sam and his friend Tony took the other bedroom, reducing it to Pompeii within an hour. Then, their work completed, they shook us down for sushi money and headed out for the wild street life of Park City.

The thing about Easter is that Jesus comes back from the dead both resurrected and broken, with the wounds from the nails still visible. People needed to see that it really did happen, the brutality, the human death. He came back with a body—not like Casper or Topper; he didn't come back as the vague idea of a spirit returning. No, it was physical, a wounded body. He had lived, he had died; and then you could touch him, and he could eat; and these four things are as bodily as life gets.

The first thing Sue and I did was to locate an Easter Week service online, and we followed it to the book. Well, sort of, in the reform sense of "followed" and "book." That night we celebrated Maundy Thursday, when Jesus had Passover with his disciples before his arrest and gave them all communion. We used Coca-Cola for wine, and Pepperidge Farm Goldfish for the bread, broken in remembrance of him.

Then we washed each other's feet. Jesus had washed his disciples' feet, to show that peace was not about power; it was about love and gentleness, and being of service. Washing Sue's feet was scary. I did not feel like Jesus. I felt very nervous. I don't even like to wash my own feet. We put some soap in a Tupperware tub, and she sat on the couch, and I lifted her feet into the warm water and washed them gently with a soapy washcloth. And then she washed mine.

I watched Sue sleep beside me in bed off and on all night. Sometimes she was so still that I was sure she was dead. She looked like a beautiful corpse, slightly yellow, slightly smelly, ethereal. She'd snore softly, or open her eyes and look at me. "Hi, Annie," she'd say in a small voice.

In the morning after breakfast, Sue, Sam, Tony, and I took the ski lift to the summit. The boys disappeared. Sue, wearing a lavender ski jacket, had 110 pounds on her five-foot-nine frame, and she was wobbly and trembling. People turned to stare at her, because she was yellow and emaciated. She smiled; people smiled back. She had great teeth. "Oh yeah, and I used to be *built*," she said, as we got our bearings in the snow. "I used to have a *rack* on me." We stood together at the summit, looking at the mountains and an endless blue sky, and suddenly I fell over. She helped me up, and we laughed and headed down the mountain.

She hadn't been on the slopes for years, and she moved gingerly; the air was thin and she had cancer in her lungs. Then she pushed hard on her poles and took off farther down the mountain. At some point she turned around and waited for me, and as soon as I saw her, I stopped, and fell over again. There I was, sprawled in the snow, with my skis at an angle over my head, looking like Gregor Samsa in *The Metamorphosis*. She waited for me to get up and ski to where she stood, and then she taught me one of the most important things I have ever learned—how to fall better. She pointed out that when I fell, I usually didn't fall that hard. "You're so afraid of falling that it's keeping you from skiing as well as you could. It's keeping you from having fun." So each time I fell, I lay there a moment, convinced that I had broken my hip, that it was all hopeless, and she would show me how to get back up. Each time, I'd dust the snow off my butt, look over at her, and head back down the mountain. After she saw that I could fall safely, she tore off down the slope.

We celebrated Good Friday that night, a week late. It's a sad day, of loss and cruelty, and all you have to go on is faith that the light shines in the darkness, and nothing, not death, not disease, not even the government, can overcome it. I hate that you can't prove the beliefs of my faith. If I were God, I'd have the answers at the end of the workbook, so you could check as you went along, to see if you're on the right track. But nooooooo. Darkness is our context, and Easter's context: without it, you couldn't see the light. Hope is not about proving anything. It's about choosing to believe this one thing, that love is bigger than any grim, bleak shit anyone can throw at us.

After the Good Friday service, Sue wanted to show me her legs, the effects of all that skin grafting. The skin was shocking, wounded and as alien as snakeskin.

"Wow," I said. Sue let me study it awhile. "I have trouble with my cellulite," I said, guiltily.

"Yeah," she answered, "but this is what me being alive looks like now."

She had fought militantly for her body over time, but she was tender and maternal with it. She took long, hot baths at night, and then smoothed on lotions.

The next morning we celebrated Holy Saturday, the day before Easter, when Jesus was dead and hidden in the tomb, and nothing made sense, and no one knew that he was going to be alive again. Most of his disciples had left Golgotha on Good Friday even before he died; only a few women remained at the cross. The disciples skulked off like dogs to the Upper Room, to wait, depressed and drunk—or at least this is what I imagine. I certainly would have, and I would have been thinking, "We are so fucked." Father Tom adds that there was a lot of cigarette smoke that night, and Monday-morning quarterbacking.

One thing Sue wanted to do before she died was to get a massage, to be touched sensuously again, so we arranged for massages on this Saturday.

"I'll tell you," she said, as we walked to the salon, "you don't see a lot of bodies like Sue Schuler's here in Park City, Utah."

Sue got a gorgeous masseur from India—he looked like Siddhartha—while I got a tense white German woman. Sue and her masseur walked off together, and she glanced over her shoulder with the pleasure of someone on her way to her bridal suite.

My masseuse looked like she was impatient to start slapping me.

When I saw Sue again, an hour later, she smelled of aromatic lemon oils.

"Did you feel shy at all?" I asked.

"Nah!" she told me. "Not after I gave him a tour of the bod."

Sue got up early on Sunday, the day we were leaving. The sun was pouring through the windows; there was a bright blue sky. She no longer looked jaundiced. She was light brown, rosy. She made us her special apricot scones, small, light yellow, flecked with orange fruit, for breakfast. I tried to discourage her, because I didn't want her feelings to be hurt if the boys turned up their noses: "The boys won't eat apricot scones," I insisted. "They eat cereal, Pop-Tarts . . . treyf!"

"Oh, they'll eat my scones," she said slyly. And they did; we all did. We ate all but four, which she packed up for us to take on the plane. Two survived the drive to the airport in Salt Lake City. They were gone by the time we arrived home.

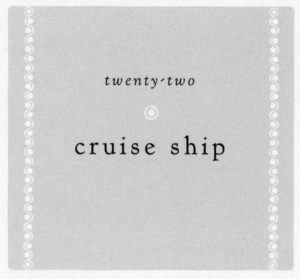

twenty-two

cruise ship

The aunties have put on weight since our last trip to the tropics, the aunties being the jiggly areas of my legs and butt that show when I put on a swimsuit. I had fallen in love with them five or six years ago, the darling aunties, shyly yet bravely walking exposed along the beaches of Huatulco, Mexico. Used to having them hidden in the dark of long pants and capris and the indoors, I suddenly understood that they had carried me through my days without complaint, strong and able, their only desire to accompany me, on beaches, in shorts, and to swim in tropical water. I vowed to include them from then on, to be as kind and grateful as possible.

But that had been nearly fifteen pounds earlier.

Now they wanted to come with me to the Caribbean.

My friends Buddy and Father Tom had persuaded me to go on a cruise with them in March 2003, shortly before the United States went to war "preemptively" in Iraq. Tom said the trip would be a lot like the cruises I take in the comfort of my own home when the world has gotten me down, left me incredulous and defeated. At those times, I make a nest for my baby self on the couch in the living room. I stretch out with a comforter and pillows, and magazines, the cat, unguents, and my favorite drink, cranberry and soda with a lime twist. These are periods of stress and Twilight Zone isolation, marked by hypochondria, numb terror, despair, and the conviction that I must go on a diet. Even at—especially at—these times, I hate to stop, though I know that to go faster and faster and do more is to move in the direction of death. Continuous movement, I tell myself, argues a wasted life. And so I try to create a cruise ship, to carry me back toward living.

The main difference between my cruise, though, and the one Tom and Buddy wanted me to go on, was that at my house, during school hours, there is no one around to whom I have to be nice, and no one who will see me in a bathing suit. And my cruise takes only two hours, instead of a week. It's unbelievably healing; it resets me. Yet it takes time, at least two hours. You can't rush a cruise ship; you can't hurry doing nothing. After a while, you see the sweetest, most invigorating thing of all: one person tenderly caring for another, even if it's just me taking care of me on my old couch.

Tom and Buddy persisted, and Sam was desperate to go, and Tom pulled some strings to arrange for nearly free passage on an Italian cruise ship. He and I would give lectures on faith to a group of sober people, in exchange for a week traveling among Caribbean ports with Buddy, Sam, and Sam's friend Alex.

Sam and Alex and I got up one day at dawn and flew to Fort Lauderdale. I had developed a tic by the time we met up with Tom and Buddy at the dock. I'm the world's worst traveler, afraid of all the usual things—of wars, of snakes, of sharks, of undertows. But I was also worried about group hugs, VX gas attacks, and huge platters of cream puffs. I was afraid I would never be able to stop eating the cream puffs once I got started: I saw myself as Al Pacino in *Scarface,* facedown on the plate of cocaine, only I'd be buried in puff pastry, custard in my hair.

I love to swim in warm seas but hate getting there. I cling to the motto of my favorite travel agents, Karl and Carl, who advise, "Trust no one, see nothing."

A thousand people were waiting to board when we arrived at the dock. The predominant adornment—stitched, beaded, embossed, tattooed—was the U.S. flag. There were lots of women with big hair, but as Ann Richards once said, "The bigger the hair, the closer to heaven." My sense, which was confirmed in conversations later in the week, was that these were not people with a lot of money: these were largely people who saved to go on cruises every few years.

Tom was wearing a T-shirt with the Arabic alphabet on it. Buddy had a bag of M&M's, and the five of us ate them by the fistful. Tom and Buddy, in their upscale hobo clothes and with the beginnings of beards, stuck out in the bright, cheery crowd. People gave Buddy second looks, because he's the last person you'd expect to find on a cruise ship, besides me. He's in his mid-fifties, and to the untrained eye looks sort of seedy: overweight, with fly-away hair and at least two front teeth missing, as if he'd just gotten out of bed and forgotten his partial dentures.

Tom travels worldwide to lead spiritual retreats and teach English, and very little worries him when it comes to travel. Buddy, in contrast, had not been on a boat since the Vietnam War, and everything waterish scares him. As soon as we were safely onboard, he became convinced that the ship would tip over. Then, after we were shown to our rooms by smiling, handsome young men, he became convinced that a revolution was brewing among the cabin help. And that John Ashcroft was spying on us three adults, because of Tom's shirt, and also because, while standing in line in port, we had accidentally expressed our opinions on George Bush's sobriety and deft diplomatic touch in the Middle East.

Sam and Alex went off on their own, and we went to sit outside and look out at the ocean, which was kindergarten blue. People streamed past us in bright-colored leisure wear and with flags—flag pins, T-shirts, purses, sarongs, swimsuits, baseball caps, fingernails. A woman with a huge blond beehive wrapped in a flag scarf walked by, and Buddy turned to Tom with a look of horror. "Live and let live," said Tom. "The rain and the sun fall on the just and unjust, and while this is offensive, it is true."

I loved my room. It was small and clean and had a porthole—and there was no one else in it. I could have stayed there forever, if I hadn't been in there with myself.

I started to channel Buddy: worried about the ship's tipping over, water pouring through my porthole, shark attacks. I put on some shorts and announced to the aunties that we were going for a brisk walk on the ship's promenade. They are so in love with me, as if I were a gentleman caller. Half the time I am hard on them, viewing them with contempt, covering them in blue jeans when it is hot, threatening to do something drastic one of these days—I'll make them start jogging, that's what I'll do! Or I'll get them some lymphatic seaweed wraps, bandage them like mummies in Saran Wrap, and then parboil them for an hour. Sometimes I catch myself being mean to them, and my heart softens, and I apologize, hang my head, and put lotion on them, as if laying on hands. And after periods when I have acted most ashamed of them, I adorn them with children's tattoo bandages, with butterflies and wolves.

◉

Sam and Alex became co-conspirators with Buddy on our way to dinner the first night, after he announced to them, sotto voce, that he had discovered plans for an uprising among the cabin crew, brewing, even as we walked, in the boiler room. After that, the boys would follow him anywhere.

On the way to the dining room, Buddy took us on a tour of the ship's more glaring infirmities: gouges in the wall, various cracks that needed caulking. He showed us to the fancy glass elevators in the center of the ship, from which people were streaming on their way to the dining rooms, past well-appointed shops and bars, ornate columns and marble staircases. When everyone had gotten out of one elevator, Buddy stared inside and clutched his head. He looked at Sam and Alex to see if they had noticed: the handrail had pulled free, and screws stuck out of the walls. "What if the *hull* is like this?" he said. Alex and Sam gripped their foreheads.

I walked to dinner with my arm on Buddy's, like royalty, past the shops, where vendors stood in the doorways and called for us to come in, like the sirens in the *Odyssey*. Buddy, with his missing front teeth and mussed-up hair, pulled me close, protectively. "This woman is *incorruptible*!" he cried to them.

There was way too much food on the cruise, every time you turned around. Half of me wanted to eat it all, and half wanted to go on a diet. I heard my therapist reminding me again and again that diets make you fat and crazy, ninety-five percent of the time. So I asked the aunties, who get out so rarely, what *they* wanted to eat. They covered their mouths; it was too ridiculous to say. Eventually they chose slices of mango, cocktail prawns, and whole-wheat buns still hot from the oven, and two servings of crème brûlée.

Sam and Alex wore white shirts and khakis to dinner, and the five of us sat with four adults we'd just met. I watched the other adults relate to the boys, who talked away like normal people, making shifty eye contact as they spoke; when others spoke, the boys listened. Every so often Sam looked at me with a vague scorn, as though he thought I was talking too much, but I tried to let him be. I am not here to be his friend. I'm here to be me, which is taking a great deal longer than I had hoped, and I am here to raise him to be a person of integrity and joy. Besides, the kid you know at home is only a facet of the child who lives in the world. His voice, bearing, and vibe change to suit the company, as in those flip books where you can change the hat, head, torso, and legs of the figure, so that an admiral with a spyglass can turn into a pirate, then into a sea monster, then into a sailor or a porpoise. I liked to watch Sam discover parts of himself through other people at the table, the way I have liked to watch him over the years discover Caesar salad, and the Rolling Stones, and even, to some extent, me.

"Why are you eating such weird food?" Sam demanded of Buddy, who had chosen only an appetizer and dessert, pumpkin soup and crème brûlée.

"I'm preparing for the nursing home," Buddy said, opening his eyes wide. It took a moment for Sam to realize Buddy was teasing. "I am! I practice sleeping with a pillow between my knees, so I don't get bedsores."

"Oh, Buddy," said Sam, so affectionately it was as if the flip book had just gone past the spy, past the pirate, past the hoodlum, to a young sweet boy.

◉

I met up with Tom and Buddy for breakfast the next morning. They already had been to the Internet café and were filled with the latest evidence that the United States really was about to attack Iraq within days. "The whole world hates us now, and I'm so afraid," Buddy said. "I don't feel there's any hope at all—I feel like one of those goats you see in Indonesia, that tour guides bring along with them, tied to the top of their buses, when they take people to see Komodo dragons. They toss the goats over the cliffs to the Komodo dragons below."

"*Live* goats?" I asked.

"The goats *have* to be alive, because the dragons want to play, and it's more fun for the tourists."

"Maybe the goats don't know what awaits them."

"Of course the goats know," Buddy replied. "The smell of Komodo dragon shit and dead goats gets stronger the closer they get."

"What are we going to do? I mean, seriously."

"I can't speak for you, miss," Tom said. "But I'm going back to my room pretty soon, and I'm going to stretch out and read all morning. And if there is crème brûlée again for lunch, I think I'll be able to get through the day."

That sounded like a plan. I got into bed with a stack of magazines. Tom had given me *The Nation* and *Harper's,* while the receptionist at the spa had lent me *Harper's Bazaar,* and the combination was perversely right.

After a while, though, I went to visit Tom, whose room was next door to mine. He was lying on his back, reading a book about Muslim culture.

"I get so afraid," I said.

"And God delights in you, even when you're scared and at your craziest. Just like God delights in the men in their flag bikinis, with their little units showing."

"I don't get it."

"I'm incredulous, too."

I stretched out beside him on the bed, laughing. "Some of these people seem to be drinking dozens of nice social drinks all day," I said.

"As soon as we're tied up near a beach, we'll have them all thrown overboard. After lunch, before boating. Until then, we'll just be kind and say, 'Hi! How are you doing? Can I get you another crème brûlée?'"

◉

It was beautiful and dreamy up on deck. I lounged on a chair in the shade, in my shorts, studying the people who were lying in direct sun. I heard my father's dermatologist explaining to him, thirty years ago, "A tan skin is a damaged skin," when he was treating him for melanoma. I practiced identifying with a few people nearby, but not the thin, lithe, young, tanned, toned beauties. What was the point? It was like a caribou's comparing herself with a cat, a different species altogether. That's me in twenty pounds, I thought pleasantly, looking at one woman. That's me in twenty years, I thought, watching an old man with Coke-bottle glasses. I closed my eyes and listened to the engines, and to distant voices. I felt as though I were inside a great breathing being, buoyed up by the water in the pool, the pool buoyed up by the ocean, floating on the earth. I remembered learning to swim in the deep end of the rec center pool, when my dad would hold me up until I felt safe enough to rest down into the water and float. In those days, we all spent too much time in the sun—who knew?

I slathered on more sunscreen, pulled my floppy lavender hat down lower, and covered my legs with a towel, even though I was in shade.

I slept and woke a few times over the next hour. Once when I came to, a bevy of young women was swimming in the pool, so sunlit and Pepsodent and similar that for a groggy moment I thought they were doing synchronized swimming. They stirred my memory of the older girls at the rec center, the thirteen- and fourteen-year-olds, practicing in the deep end while we younger girls paddled nearby, agog, flannel fish sewn to our suits so the lifeguards would know we could swim. We worshipped the peppy, vigorous older girls in their white tank suits and bathing caps with petals and chin straps, swimming on their backs in perfect circles like a dream, like a wedding cake, suddenly dipping beneath the turquoise water, the pointed stalks of their legs reappearing first, and then the rest of them, as they floated on their backs like skydivers in a daisy chain.

When I was young, I thought that this must be what heaven was like, to be one of those teens. When you're synchronized, you are all beautiful—Breck girls opening and closing like anemones in time-lapse photography, kaleidoscopically.

I fell asleep again, and when I woke, Buddy was standing over me, calling my name. Sam was peering at me with disapproval, as if he'd found me sunbathing in biohazard gear. Buddy bent down beside me.

"Things are clearly growing uglier down in the boiler room," Buddy whispered. "We need to be on the lookout for possible security breaches."

"Who's the leader of the uprising?" I asked.

"The revolution is being led by unseen forces. In the boiler room."

Alex held his finger to his lips. I nodded grimly.

◉

Tom and I were out on deck that afternoon, waiting for Buddy. Everything was more fun when he was around. Sam and Alex had fallen in with a roving gaggle of teenagers, had gone off to God knows where.

"Why are you always chewing on ice?" I asked.

"Rage," said Tom.

293

"I'm worried about what Sam and Alex do after we go to sleep," I said. "I'm afraid they sneak into the bars. It's such a mean, scary world. And Sam can be so mean to me, too."

"He's very different with us from how he is with you. He's wonderful with us. All kids' behavior makes their parents a little crazy sometimes. And vice versa. My ninety-four-year-old mother said something annoying to me over the phone on Christmas Eve, and I whined at her, 'I *hate* it when you say that.' So she says it again, right? I said, 'Please don't say that. It makes me feel like an eleven-year-old.' And when she said it again, I slammed down the phone. She's ninety-four! I'm a middle-aged priest—and it's Christmas Eve! I wanted to throttle her over the phone. But I finally figured out that it was *my* craziness, so I went to see her at the old folks' home, and I brought everyone communion, and it was lovely."

We stood at the railing, our backs to the sea. Even from fifteen feet up, I could see the corrugated skin, the lumps and veins and chicken-skin knees of other passengers. I saw huge guts, bad moles. There were many fat, hairy middle-aged men in teeny bikinis, many matronly middle-aged women with big fallen breasts and poor posture—that which used to be the offering was now the burden. But it's our hearts that weigh us down. Who could even imagine what cargo these people carried? One old woman seemed to be wearing oversize pink-tinted panty hose. They looked like the pink tights we wore for ballet lessons, a room of small girls in black leotards, leaping about the rec center's deeply scratched polished floors. Because I was so thin, my tights were always baggy, but I felt pretty—until I would hear a grown-up ask my mother, "Don't you ever feed her?" and my mother would laugh, as if this was so witty, even though we heard it all the time. But she'd be mad when she told my father later. He always used the word "slender" to describe me. The pink stockings on the cruise ship turned out to be the old woman's own skin. She had grown too thin for her tights, and they were bagging on her.

Saint Bette said that heaven is where people finally stop talking about their weight and what they look like. I feel grateful just to think of Bette Midler's being alive during my years on the planet—just as I do about Michael Jordan and Nelson Mandela. Gratitude, not understanding, is the secret to joy and equanimity. I prayed for the willingness to have very mild spiritual well-being. I didn't need to understand the hypostatic unity of the Trinity; I just needed to turn my life over to whoever came up with

redwood trees. And in a sudden moment of clarity, I realized that I also needed to create my own cruise ship again.

I said good-bye to Tom, and stopped at the snack bar
for a glass of cranberry juice and soda with lime. I went by
the café and asked the aunties what they might like for a
snack—bread pudding or fruit salad. They wanted half a
sandwich, a lot of bread pudding, and one small whole-
wheat bun. I think they would have ordered a bread bev-
erage if they could—beer, with hops and barley, or in the
interest of sobriety, a raisin-bread frappé. Bread is as spiritual as human life gets. Rumi wrote, "Be a well-baked
loaf." Loaves are made to be eaten, to be buttered, and
shared. Rumi is saying to be of service, to be delicious and
give life.

The aunties know things.

I went to my room, changed into my swimsuit,
slathered on sunscreen, and stopped at the spa for a couple of magazines. I went on deck, where people lay sunbathing. I found a lounge chair in the shade and lay down.
At first I used my towel as a blanket, but even in the shade
it was hot, and the aunties felt smothered. They love the
sun. So I took off the towel, and then my shorts, and ate
my bread pudding. I opened a magazine. Every so often, I
looked up and smiled at people walking by.

Once again: If Jesus was right, these are all my brothers and sisters.

And they are *so* letting themselves go.

This is not how Jesus would have seen things, but at first I couldn't help it—once again I saw an expanse of walruses, big wet bodies flopped down on towels, letting it all hang out. Some people were sleeping in the sun. I worried about their sunburns and melanomas, as some of them had moles I thought should be looked at when we reached the next port. People were putting cool lotion on their bodies, and on one another. They got up and returned with drinks. They handed one another caps and visors, and covered one another with towels.

I drank my cranberry and soda, and put more lotion on the aunties. They loved it out here on deck—the sun, our favorite drink, watching the company onboard. I felt safe with the people around me now. This sense of safety suddenly made it clear to me that, looking at us, God saw not walruses but babies: radiant and befuddled, all these hearts at temporary rest. When you rest, you catch your breath, and it fills your lungs and holds you up, like water wings, like my father in the deep end of the rec center pool.

twenty-three

let us
commence

I am honored and surprised when people ask me to speak at their graduations, and this is what I say:

This must be a magical day for you. I wouldn't know. I accidentally forgot to graduate from college. I meant to, thirty-some years ago, but things got away from me. I did graduate from high school—do I get a partial credit for that?—although, unfortunately, my father had forgotten to pay the book bill, so at the graduation ceremony, when I opened the case to look at my diploma, it was empty. Except for a ransom note that said, See Mrs. Foley, the bookkeeper, if you ever want to see your diploma alive again.

I went to Goucher College in Maryland for the best possible reason—to learn—but dropped out at nineteen for the best possible reason—to become a writer. Those of you who have read my work know that instead, I accidentally became a Kelly Girl for a while. Then, in a dazzling career move, I got hired as a clerk-typist in the Nuclear Quality Assurance Department at Bechtel, where I worked typing and sorting triplicate forms. I hate to complain, but it was not very stimulating work. However, it paid the bills, so I could write my stories every night when I got home. I worked at Bechtel for six months— but I swear I had nothing to do with the company's involvement in the Bush administration's shameless war profiteering. I just sorted triplicate forms.

It was a terrible job, at which I did a terrible job, but it paid $600 a month, which, augmented by food stamps, was enough to pay my rent and grocery bills. This is a real problem if you are crazy enough to want to be an artist— you have to give up your dreams of swimming pools and fish forks, and take any old job. At twenty, I was hired as an assistant editor at a magazine; I think that was the last real job I've had.

I bet I'm beginning to make some parents nervous— here I am, bragging of being a dropout, and unemployable, and about to make a pitch for you to follow your creative dreams, when what parents want is for their children to do well in their field, to make them look good, and maybe also to assemble a tasteful fortune.

But that is not your problem. Your problem is how you are going to spend this one odd and precious life you have been issued. Whether you're going to live it trying to look good and creating the illusion that you have power over people and circumstances, or whether you are going to taste it, enjoy it, and find out the truth about who you are.

At some point I started getting published, and experienced a meager knock-kneed standing in the literary world, and I started to get almost everything that many of you graduates are hoping for—except for the money. I got a lot of things that society had promised would make me whole and fulfilled—all the things that the culture tells you, from preschool on, will quiet the throbbing anxiety inside you. I got some stature, the respect of other writers, even a low-grade fame. The culture says these things will save you, as long as you also manage to keep your weight down. But the culture lies.

Slowly, after dozens of rejection slips and failures and false starts and postponed dreams—what Langston Hughes called dreams deferred—I stepped onto the hallowed ground of being a published novelist, and then, fifteen years later, I started to make real money.

I'd wanted to be a writer my whole life. But when I finally made it, I felt like a greyhound catching the mechanical rabbit she'd been chasing for so long—discovering it was merely metal, wrapped up in cloth. It wasn't alive; it had no spirit. It was fake. Fake doesn't feed anything. Only spirit feeds spirit, your own and the universal spirit, in the same way that only your own blood type, and O negative, the universal donor, can sustain you. "Making it" had nothing that could slake the thirst I had for immediacy, and connection.

From the wise old pinnacle of my years, I can tell you that what you're looking for is already inside you. You've heard this before, but the holy thing inside you really is that which causes you to seek it. You can't buy it, lease it, rent it, date it, or apply for it. The best job in the world can't give it to you. Neither can success, or fame, or financial security—besides which, there ain't no such thing. John D. Rockefeller was once asked, "How much money is enough?" and he answered, "Just a little bit more."

It can be confusing—most of your parents want you to do well, to be successful. They want you to be happy—or at least happyish. And they want you to be nicer to them, just a little nicer—*is that so much to ask?*

They want you to love, and be loved, and find peace, and laugh and find meaningful work. But they also— some of them, a few of them (not yours—yours are fine) —they also want you to chase the bunny for a while. To get ahead, sock some money away, and then find a balance between the bunny chase and savoring your life.

But you don't know whether you're going to live long enough to slow down, relax, and have fun, and discover the truth of your spiritual identity. You may not be des- tined to live a long life; you may not have sixty more years to discover and claim your own deepest truth. As Breaker Morant said, you have to live every day as if it's your last, because one of these days, you're bound to be right.

It might help if I go ahead and tell you what I think is the truth of your spiritual identity. . . .

Actually, I don't have a clue.

I do know you are not what you look like, or how much you weigh, or how you did in school, or whether you start a job next Monday or not. Spirit isn't what you do, it's . . . well, again, I don't actually know. They proba- bly taught this junior year at Goucher; I should have stuck around. But I know that you feel it best when you're not doing much—when you're in nature, when you're very quiet or, paradoxically, listening to music.

I know you can feel it and hear it in the music you love, in the bass line, in the harmonies, in the silence between notes: in Chopin and Eminem, Emmylou Harris, Neil Young, Bach, whomever. You can close your eyes and feel the divine spark concentrated in you, like a little Dr. Seuss firefly. It flickers with life and relief, like an American in a foreign country who suddenly hears someone speaking English. In the Christian tradition, they say that the soul rejoices in hearing what it already knows. And so you pay attention when that Dr. Seuss creature inside you sits up and strains to hear.

We can see Spirit made visible when people are kind to one another, especially when it's a really busy person, like you, taking care of a needy, annoying, neurotic person, like you. In fact, that's often when we see Spirit most brightly.

It's magic to see Spirit, largely because it's so rare. Mostly you see the masks and the holograms that the culture presents as real. You see how you're doing in the world's eyes, or your family's, or—worst of all—yours, or in the eyes of people who are doing better than you— much better than you—or worse. But you are not your bank account, or your ambition. You're not the cold clay lump you leave behind when you die. You're not your collection of walking personality disorders. You are Spirit, you are love, and even though it is hard to believe sometimes, you are free. You're here to love, and be loved, freely. If you find out next week that you are terminally ill—and we're all terminally ill on this bus—what will matter are memories of beauty, that people loved you, and that you loved them.

So how do we feed and nourish our spirit, and the spirit of others?

First find a path, and a little light to see by. Then push up your sleeves and start helping. Every single spiritual tradition says that you must take care of the poor, or you are so doomed that not even Jesus or the Buddha can help you.

You don't have to go overseas. There are people in this country who are poor in spirit, worried, depressed, dancing as fast as they can; their kids are sick, or their retirement savings are gone. There is great loneliness among us, life-threatening loneliness. People have given up on peace, on equality. They've even given up on the Democratic Party, which I haven't, not by a long shot. You do what you can, what good people have always done: you bring thirsty people water, you share your food, you try to help the homeless find shelter, you stand up for the underdog.

I secretly believe that this makes Jesus love you more.

Anything that can help you get your sense of humor back feeds the spirit, too. In the Bill Murray movie *Stripes,* a very tense army recruit announces during his platoon's introductions: "The name's Francis Sawyer, but everybody calls me Psycho. Any of you guys call me Francis, and I'll kill you. . . . And I don't like nobody touching me. Any of you homos touch me, and I'll kill you." The sergeant responds, "Lighten up, Francis." So you may need to upgrade your friends. You need to find people who laugh gently at themselves, who remind you gently to lighten up.

Rest and laughter are the most spiritual and subversive acts of all. Laugh, rest, slow down. Some of you start jobs on Monday; some of you wish you did—some of your parents are asthmatic with anxiety that you don't. They shared this with me before the ceremony began.

But again, this is not your problem. If your parents are hell-bent for someone in your family to make a name in the field of, say, molecular cell biology, then maybe when you're giving them a final tour of campus you can show them to the admissions office.

I would recommend that you all take a long deep breath, and stop. Just be where your butts are, and breathe. Take some time. You are graduating today. Refuse to cooperate with anyone who is trying to shame you into hopping right back up onto the rat exercise wheel.

Rest, but pay attention. Refuse to cooperate with anyone who is stealing your freedom, your personal and civil liberties, and then smirking about it. I'm not going to name names.

But slow down. Better yet, lie down.

In my twenties I devised a school of relaxation that has unfortunately fallen out of favor in the ensuing years—it was called Prone Yoga. You just lay around as much as possible. You could read, listen to music, you could space out or sleep. But you had to be lying down. Maintaining the prone.

You've graduated. You have nothing left to prove, and besides, it's a fool's game. If you agree to play, you've already lost. It's Charlie Brown and Lucy, with the football. If you keep getting back on the field, they win. There are so many great things to do right now. Write. Sing. Rest. Eat cherries. Register voters. And—oh my God—I nearly forgot the most important thing: Refuse to wear uncomfortable pants, even if they make you look really thin. Promise me you'll never wear pants that bind or tug or hurt, pants that have an opinion about how much you've just eaten. The pants may be lying! There is way too much lying and scolding going on politically right now without having your pants get in on the act, too.

So bless you. You've done an amazing thing. And you are loved; you are capable of lives of great joy and meaning. It's what you are made of. And it's what you're here for. Take care of yourselves; take care of one another.

And give thanks, like this: *Thank* you.

twenty-four

market street

I woke up full of hate and fear the day before a recent peace march in San Francisco. This was disappointing, as I'd hoped to wake up feeling somewhere between the sad elegance of Virginia Woolf, and Wavy Gravy. Instead, I was angry that our country's leaders had bullied and bought their way into preemptive war. Hitting first has always been the mark of evil. I don't think one great religious or spiritual thinker has ever said otherwise. Everyone, from almost every tradition, agrees on five things. Rule 1: We are all family. Rule 2: You reap exactly what you sow, that is, you cannot grow tulips from zucchini seeds. Rule 3: Try to breathe every few minutes or so. Rule 4: It helps beyond words to plant bulbs in the dark of winter. Rule 5: It is immoral to hit first.

I tried to pray my way out of the fear and hate, but my mind was once again a pinball machine of blame and hopelessness. I had planted bulbs a few months before, but they had not bloomed yet, and I did not want to get out of bed. Like everyone I knew, I was despondent about the war. And I wondered if I actually even believed in God anymore. It seemed ridiculous, this conviction that I had an invisible partner in life, and that we were all part of a bigger, less punishing and isolated truth. I lay there gnashing my teeth, sure that what you see is what you get. This was it. This earth, this country, here, now, was all there was. This was where all life happened, the up and the down and the plus and the minus and the world of choices and consequences. Not an easy place, but a place full of significance.

I clutched my cat as I used to when my parents fought, a life preserver in cold, deep water.

But then—a small miracle—I started to believe in George Bush. I really did: In my terror, I wondered whether maybe he was smarter than we think he is, and had grasped classified intelligence and nuance in a way that was well above my own understanding or that of our era's most brilliant thinkers.

Then I thought: Wait—George *Bush?* And relief washed over me like gentle surf, because believing in George Bush was so ludicrous that believing in God seems almost rational.

I decided to start from scratch, with a simple prayer: "Hi!" I said.

Someone or something hears. I don't know much about its nature, only that when I cry out, it hears, and moves closer to me, and I don't feel so alone. I feel better. And I felt better that morning, starting over. No shame in that—Augustine said that you have to start your relationship with God all over from the beginning, every day. Yesterday's faith does not wait for you like a dog with your slippers and the morning paper in its mouth. You seek it, and in seeking it, you find it. During the Renaissance, Fra Giovanni Giocondo wrote:

> *No heaven can come to us unless our hearts find rest*
> *in it today. Take heaven!*
> *No peace lies in the future which is not hidden in*
> *this present little instant. Take peace!*

And so I roused myself and went to meet some friends in San Francisco.

We milled around the Embarcadero, where you could see endless sky and ocean, and a Möbius strip of the '60s, a massive crowd gathered once again on sacred ground. Haranguers harangued us from various sound systems unimproved in the last thirty-five years, like heavy metal played backward at the wrong speed. But the energy and signs and faces of the crowd were an intoxicating balm, and by some marvelous yogic stretch, we all stopped trying to figure out whom and what we agreed with, and who the bad elements were: The socialist haranguers? The Punx for Peace, who had come prepared with backpacks full of rocks? The Israel haters? The right-wing Zionists? You just had to let go, because Market Street was wide enough for us all, and we began to march, each a small part of one big body, fascinatingly out of control, like protoplasm bobbing along.

The sea of people looked like a great heartbroken circus, wild living art, motley and stylish, old and young, lots of Buddhists, people from unions and churches and temples, punks and rabbis and aging hippies and nuns and veterans—God, I love the Democratic Party—strewn together on the asphalt lawn of Market Street. We took small shuffle steps, like Zen monks in a crowded wedding procession. It was like being on a conveyer belt, overwhelming and scary, because you might trip and get stepped on, but once you were really on the street, you could sit by the curb and sob, or adjust to it. It's disturbing to not walk with your usual gait, to move at once so slowly and with such purpose. I felt I was trying to pat my head and rub my stomach at the same time.

The "I" turned into "we." You shuffled along with your friends, moving at the pace of the whole organization, moving to the heartbeat of the percussion. You saw people you knew, and hung out awhile, and then they moved away, and new people fell in step beside you, and offered you comments and gum. Whoever came along came along. The goodwill gave you a feeling of safety in this mob, a fizzy euphoria despite the grim reality of these times. Songs I've loved for decades were sung—"We Shall Not Be Moved," "Study War No More," "Give Peace a Chance"—and then we'd tromp along, and the peace-march wave rose again, a joyful roar of solidarity rippling out from the front, over us, then picked up by those behind.

There was gaping, and a lot of volition; you were swept along, but the crowd had a self-correcting mechanism—it kept letting go of what wasn't quite right, the more raw, angry elements, the strident and divisive. It was a Golden Rule parade—you acted the way you wish the government would act, with goodness, and tender respect, and this held the peace. The splinter groups that went crazy later and trashed everything were peaceful when they were with us. I saw only friendliness, sorrow, goodness, and great theater. My favorites were the people dressed as sheep on stilts, who resembled huge silver masked-ball aliens, with horns and curly tinsel wool, like puppets that Louis XIV might have commissioned. No one had any idea why they were sheep, or why they were on stilts. Maybe they were peace sheep, and maybe they just wanted to see better.

The Women in Black moved solemnly in the middle of the throng, steadfast and profound, witnessing for peace. They dressed in black, like the Madres in South America. They stopped you with their presence, like punctuation, made you remember why you were here.

Two things carried the day: regular people saying no to power, and glorious camaraderie. We were sad and afraid, and we had done the most radical thing of all: we had shown up, not knowing what else to do, and without much hope. This was like going on a huge picnic at the edge of the fog, hoping you would walk through to something warmer. The mantra you could hear in our voices and our footsteps was "I have a good feeling!" The undermutter was silent, spoken with a sort of Jewish shrug—"What good will it do to do nothing?"

The barricades were broken down for once, between races, colors, ages, sexes, classes, nations. There are so few opportunities for this to happen—at first, it feels like us versus them, and then you're shoulder to shoulder with thousands of people, reading one another's signs, signs that pierce you or make you laugh out loud. You rub shoulders, smell the bodies and the babies and pot and urine and incense and fear, and everyone's streaming past, including you. For once, you're part of the stream, and in that, in being part of it, you smell the pungent green shoots of hope. The feeling may be only for the moment. But it's a quantum moment: it might happen again, and spread and spread and spread; and for a moment and then another, there's no judgment, no figuring out, just an ebullient trudge, step, step, step.

People sang, and babies cried, and your feet started to hurt, and you wanted to go home, and just then the broad-bottomed Palestinian women started chanting, "This is what democracy looks like. This is what democracy looks like."

Wow: that's the prayer I said the morning after the peace march: Wow. I felt buoyed by all those people walking slowly together down Market Street, by the memory of the peacenik dogs with kerchiefs around their necks, the Mothers in Black, and the Peace Sheep. Then, amazingly, only a few days later, the very first bulbs began to bloom. Within a week, there were dozens of daffodils in the yard. When this finally happens in late winter every year, I'm astonished. I've always given up. In November and December when I plant them, I get swept up in the fantasy that the earth, after so much rain, will be rich and loamy. Planting bulbs sounds like a romantic and fun thing to do, but it never is. The earth is rocky and full of roots; it's clay, and it seems doomed and polluted, yet you dig little holes for the ugly, shriveled bulbs, throw in a handful of poppy seeds, and cover everything over, and you know you'll never see them again—it's death and clay and shrivel. Your hands are nicked from the rocks, your nails are black with soil. December and January have been so grim the last few years, and this year the power kept going out, and everyone was crazy as a rat. Yet here we are in February, with war drums and daffodils everywhere, and poppies waiting in the wings.